SPAIN

WESTVIEW PROFILES • NATIONS OF CONTEMPORARY WESTERN EUROPE

Ireland: The Challenge of Conflict and Change,
Richard B. Finnegan

Spain: From Repression to Renewal,
E. Ramón Arango

Greece, George A. Kourvetaris and
Betty A. Dobratz

Also of Interest

†*The Spanish Political System: Franco's Legacy,*
E. Ramón Arango

The Status of Gibraltar, Howard S. Levie

Portugal's Political Development: A Comparative Approach,
Walter C. Opello, Jr.

Portugal Since the Revolution: Economic and Political Perspectives,
edited by Jorge Braga de Macedo and Simon Serfaty

†Available in hardcover and paperback.

SPAIN

From Repression to Renewal

E. Ramón Arango

Westview Press / Boulder and London

Westview Profiles/Nations of Contemporary Western Europe

The photograph of Francisco Franco and Manuel Benítez is reprinted, with permission, from the *Jewish Chronicle*, Jan. 20, 1967. All photographs are courtesy of the Spanish consulate in Houston.

Cover photos:

        Winter fair and ramparts, Ávila
        The cathedral of Santiago de Compostela, La Coruña
        Fallas, La Plaza del Caudillo, Valencia

Published in 1985 in the United States of America by Westview Press, Inc., 5500 Central Avenue, Boulder, Colorado 80301; Frederick A. Praeger, Publisher

Library of Congress Cataloging in Publication Data
Arango, E. Ramón (Ergasto Ramón).
  Spain, from repression to renewal.
  (Westview profiles. Nations of contemporary western
Europe)
  Includes index.
  1. Spain—Politics and government—1975–
2. Spain—History. I. Title.
DP272.A7 1985   946.08   84-27096
ISBN 0-86531-335-0

Printed and bound in the United States of America

10   9   8   7   6   5   4   3   2   1

For
J. TAYLOR ROOKS

In memory of
ERGASTO and CAROLINE ARANGO

Contents

Tables and Illustrations

1

The Setting

GEOGRAPHY OF SPAIN

Spain is haphazardly cut into regions by mountains arranged as if the creative forces of nature had gone berserk, blindly slashing the surface of the land.[1] After Switzerland, Spain is the highest country in Europe; its lowlands are limited to the valley of the Guadalquivir River, parts of the valley of the Ebro River, and a thin edge of coast along the Mediterranean and the Bay of Biscay. It is not the extreme height of the mountains, however, that gives Spain its topographical character. Its tallest peaks—the Mulacén in the Sierra Nevada, near Granada, and the Pico de Aneto in the Pyrenees—are only 11,411 ft (3,480 m) and 11,116 ft (3,390 m), yet the elevation of the Iberian peninsula is so high that the average altitude of Spain is 2,165 ft (660 m).

The Central Meseta

The dominant topographic structure of Spain is, in fact, not the mountains but the high interior tableland, the *meseta central*, which ranges from 1,700 to 2,700 ft (518 to 823 m) above sea level. The meseta is divided by the gaunt central sierras, of which the most prominent are the Sierra de Guadarrama and the Sierra de Gredos, which arch to an altitude of nearly 9,000 ft (2,743 m) from the southwest to the northeast of Madrid. The northern, smaller portion of the meseta includes the regions of Leon and Old Castile; the vast southern portion encompasses New Castile, La Mancha,

1

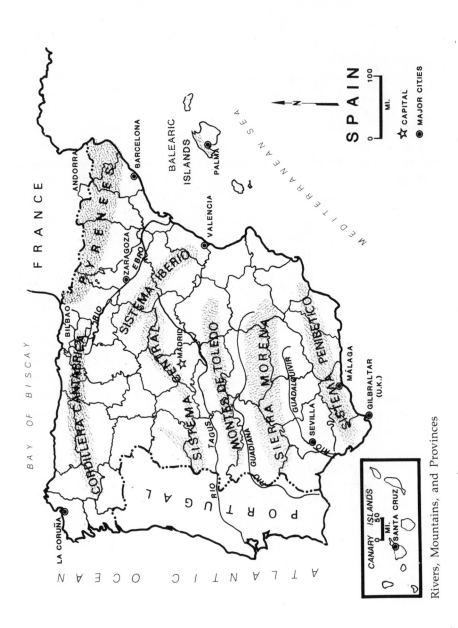

Rivers, Mountains, and Provinces

and Extremadura. This massive plateau dominates the country's geography and is responsible for the climate, the rainfall, the temperatures, and the vegetation that are the most characteristically Spanish. The meseta has also dominated Spanish history and politics, and it has influenced the national character sufficiently to make the "average" Spaniard more Castilian than Andalucian, Aragonese, Galician, Catalan, or Basque.

The meseta is a relentless and uninviting land where life for the most part has been a basic and elemental struggle to survive. It constitutes the major part of what is called "dry Spain," and most of the plateau receives no more than 20 in. (51 cm) of rainfall a year. The "continental" climate produces intensely hot summers and bitterly cold winters, with wide variations of temperature between day and night during both seasons. January lows average about 34°F (1.2°C); in the summer, temperatures often rise to 100° F (37.7° C) at midday and then drop to 70° F (21.2° C) during the night. Sparse and stunted *matorral* is the natural vegetation of the parched tableland. Where there is sufficient water, evergreen shrubs may grow as well, and stands of dwarf oak and conifers form modest woodlands in some areas. Where water is scarce, so is plant life. Wheat is the primary cultivated crop, and potatoes, barley, and rye are grown in certain areas. In La Mancha around Valdepeñas, extensive vineyards produce large quantitites of undistinguished wine. Sheep, goats, and pigs are raised on the meseta, but the most exotic livestock is the fighting bull, bred there, as in Andalucia, for the ring.

Andalucia and the Guadalquivir River Valley

The meseta ends in the south at the Sierra Morena. Between these mountains, which for centuries impeded movement to and from the meseta, and the Betic Cordillera, which defines the southern Mediterranean coast and includes the Sierra Nevada, lies the valley of the Guadalquivir River in the region of Andalucia. This is Arab Spain, today's tourist Spain. The color and vibrance that the casual traveler mistakenly associates with all of the country is found here, and also the fishers of Spain, and the waters off Galicia furnish the extraordinarily varied fish and shellfish that make Spaniards the largest consumers of seafood in Europe.

The Ebro River Valley

Between the Pyrenees to the north and the massive and forbidding Iberian Mountains to the south lies the trough carved by the Ebro River, which drops from its source in the Cantabrian Mountains to empty into the Mediterranean south of Barcelona. In general, the climate of the valley is continental, like that of the central meseta, and the seasonal and unreliable rainfall is rarely heavier than 16 in. (41 cm) a year. The scanty natural vegetation is due to this aridity, and much of the landscape is badlands, with deeply furrowed and fantastically shaped hills cut by watercourses called *arroyos*, which are dry except in flood times. With irrigation, however, certain areas of the valley are fertile, and the huertas of Zaragoza and Lérida, like those in the Guadalquivir Valley, are extremely productive. With proper protection against the cold, these huertas are able to grow almost any crop that does well in Spain, including subtropicals; the Rioja basin in the upper valley produces the finest table wine in Spain.

The Levant

The Levant is the purest Mediterranean region of Spain. It lies along the eastern coast from the mouth of the Ebro River south to the Cabo de Gata below Almeria. Like the meseta and Andalucia, the Levant is a part of dry Spain, with annual rainfall between 15 and 25 in. (38 to 63.5 cm), but between Cabo de Nao, halfway between Valencia and Alicante, and Cabo de Gata, precipitation decreases so dramatically that dry becomes semiarid, with rainfall no more than 4 to 5 in. (10.2 to 12.7 cm), the lowest in Europe. The semiarid zone is like a small piece of North Africa in Europe. The climate and vegetation resemble that of Andalucia, but average temperatures drop as one moves north toward Catalonia, and in the semiarid zone, esparto grass replaces scrub as the most common natural plant. Cultivated vegetation grows close to streams or in irrigated huertas like the ones found in the Guadalquivir and Ebro valleys. Murcia, Lorca, and Alicante are major huertas, and the huerta of Valencia contains probably the richest soil in Spain. Crops include tobacco, cotton, noncitrus and citrus fruits, almonds, sugar, rice, cereals, olives, grapes, mulberries, and hemp, but dates are the unique crop, grown in Elche in the oasis-like Huerta del Cura, the largest grove of date palms on the European continent. Gazing at the Huerta del Cura, an unknowing visitor might well believe this land to be Arabia.

THE PEOPLE

The origin of the earliest inhabitants of Spain remains mysterious. No one knows how the Basques got to Spain or from where they came; no one is certain where the Iberians came from or who they were. Anthropologists speculate that the present-day Basques are perhaps the descendants of a primitive Cro-Magnon people who lived in the Pyrenees and along the shore of the Bay of Biscay. Scholars feel more certain that the Iberians were Hamites from Saharan Africa.

The Phoenicians are the first people who can be accurately accounted for historically. They came in the eleventh century B.C. from what today would be Syria and Lebanon, attracted by the copper, gold, mercury, and silver in what is now Andalucia. The Phoenicians came primarily as traders, not as colonists, yet they lived along the southern Atlantic and Mediterranean coasts of Spain for almost six centuries. The Greeks arrived in the eighth century B.C. Like the Phoenicians before them, they came to trade and to exploit mineral wealth, but they also brought agricultural skills with them and, it is believed, introduced the grape and the olive. The Greeks produced the first written accounts of Spain, based in part on Phoenician chronicles, and the earliest existing Spanish works of art have strong Hellenic characteristics.

The Celts came to Spain from their homeland along the Rhine while the Phoenicians and Greeks were moving into the south. The Celts, however, came to stay. They arrived in two waves—the first about 1,000 B.C. and the second about

600 B.C.—and moved along the Cantabrian coast. They settled in Galicia, which even today remains the racially purest Celtic region in Spain. Eventually, the Celts spread into the center of the peninsula, where they encountered fierce opposition from the native Iberians. Over time, fighting gave way to marriage, and the union of these two peoples produced the first major ancestor of the modern Spaniard: the Celtiberian. The creation of the Celtiberian "people" was only a racial union, however; there was no concomitant sociopolitical amalgamation.

The Carthaginians arrived in Spain in 573 B.C. Invited by the Phoenicians to aid in the defense of Cádiz, the Carthaginians stayed to conquer their hosts and eventually to absorb them. Like the Phoenicians and the Greeks, the Carthaginians came primarily as traders, but they remained in Spain for almost four centuries until their civilization throughout the Mediterranean was destroyed by the Romans in the Punic Wars. Altamira wrote that Rome brought political, social, linguistic, and juridical unification to Spain.[2] One could add that Rome also brought the beginnings of religious unification, following the conversion of Constantine in 312. Rome subordinated and disciplined the peoples inhabiting Spain under a central authority sitting in Rome, and built the roads that ended isolation and contributed to the formation of a uniform culture disseminated by Latin, the single official and common language.[3] Not all of the regions of the peninsula were Romanized to the same degree nor at the same pace, but in time the socialization was so complete that it produced a new people—the Hispano-Roman, the second major ancestor of the modern Spaniard.

The union of Romans and Celtiberians created the racial mainstream of Spain. The Basques have been present since the mixing began; they have constituted a major tributary to the mainstream and not a totally separate and unalloyed ethnic group, as some extremists contend today. Even if, because of geographic isolation, the Basques in their homeland have maintained a clearer racial identity than most other Spaniards, they must still be considered Spanish. This reality makes the demands of present-day separatists something less than authentic. In the same way, the Galicians are also Spanish in spite of the geographic isolation that has given the modern Galician a purer Celtic heritage than the rest of the Spaniards, for whom the Celts make up only a part of their ancestry.

The Visigoths, who invaded and conquered Spain in 414 following the collapse of the Roman Empire, were soon absorbed by an overwhelmingly Hispano-Roman society, and it would be virtually impossible to isolate their descendants today. Moreover, the northern European physical characteristics that might identify them—height and skin and hair coloring primarily—were already present in the Spaniards because of the Celts.

The Moors, who ended Visigothic rule in Spain, are a different story. They lived in Spain from 711 to 1492, not just in the south, where their civilization flourished, but at various times during the nearly 800 years in territories throughout most of the peninsula. Intermarriage among Christians and Muslims was not uncommon, and it would be difficult to find many Spaniards today (with the possible exception of the Galicians and the Basques) who do not have Moorish ancestors.

During the century that followed the end of the Reconquest in 1492 those Muslims who would not renounce their religion were expelled from Spain. Those who rejected Islam and stayed were absorbed into the Spanish mainstream and lost both their racial and religious identity. The Jews, who had constituted a major ethnic minority throughout both Muslim and Christian Spain and whose erudition and talent had contributed incalculably to both cultures, had already been ordered out of the country by an edict of Ferdinand and Isabella in 1492.

Since the end of the Reconquest Spain's racial and religious composition has remained virtually unchanged. In modern times the country has not attracted immigrants in sufficient numbers to alter the ethnic makeup. Since 1609, when the last Muslims left the peninsula, Spain has had no religious subcultures. The Reformation did not come to Spain (the Jesuits saw to that), and Protestantism has never taken root. Even today, when more and more Spaniards no longer practice their faith, those who lapse do not embrace other religions; there are only roughly 100,000 Protestants and 12,000 Jews in Spain.[4] In fact, most of those Spaniards who no longer attend mass have been married in the church, will probably be buried from the church, and allow their children to be baptized in the church.

The decline in the practice of Catholicism in post-Franco Spain can be attributed in large part to the Spanish church's history of support for autocratic or authoritarian regimes. The failure to embrace other religions can be explained in part by the cultural identity that links being Spanish to being Catholic. In part, the failure can be attributed to the secularization that has taken place in all Western societies during the past century. As Spain moves into the European mainstream it should not be surprising to witness the erosion of religious faith among the people. The exodus from the farms, the rejection of rural and small-town life where the priest loomed so large, and the growth of cities have contributed to secularization. The demands of the burgeoning middle class for instant gratification fly in the face of asceticism and forbearance taught for centuries in Spanish classrooms and pulpits. Moreover, modern capitalism is so far removed from its links to Protestantism—in the way Max Weber and R. H. Tawney explained—that Spain's neocapitalism will likely see no growth in Protestantism to rationalize its economic posture. Spain is becoming *athée*, the way the French use the term, not atheist but unconcerned with God.

NOTES

1. See Juan Vilá Valentí, *La Península Ibérica* (Barcelona: Editorial Ariel, 1980), ch. 2.

2. Rafael Altamira, *A History of Spain* (New York: Van Nostrand Company, 1949), ch. 3.

3. Eventually, popular speech corrupted the official language, and out of that corruption grew the major languages of modern Spain: Castilian (what is today called Spanish), Galician, and Catalan.

4. *The Statesman's Year-Book* (New York: St. Martin's Press, 1983).

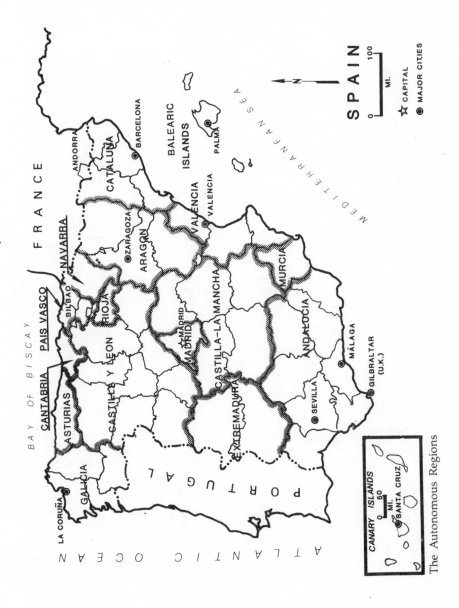

The Autonomous Regions

Table 1.1
Regions and Provinces

Spain
Population: 37,746,260
Area: 194,897 sq miles (504,782 sq km)

1. Andalucia

Population: 6,441,755
Area: 33,836.4 sq miles (87,260 sq km)
Provinces: Almeria, Cadiz, Cordoba, Granada,
Huelva, Jaen, Malaga, Seville.

2. Aragon

Population: 1,213,099
Area: 18,404 sq miles (47,669 sq km)
Provinces: Huesca, Teruel, Zaragoza.

3. Asturias

Population: 1,127,007
Area: 4,078.2 sq miles (10,563 sq km)

4. Baleares (Balearic Islands)

Population: 685,088
Area: 1,935.8 sq miles (5,014 sq km)

5. Canarias (Canary Islands)

Population: 1,444,626
Area: 2,808 sq miles (7,273 sq km)
Provinces: Las Palma, Santa Cruz de
Tenerife.

6. Cantabria

Population: 510,816
Area: 2,038.5 sq miles (5,280 sq km)

7. Castile-Leon

Population: 2,577,105
Area: 32,376.6 sq miles (83,860 sq km)
Provinces: Avila, Burgos, Leon, Palencia,
Salamanca, Segovia, Soria,
Valladolid, Zamora.

8. Castile-La Mancha

Population: 1,628,005
Area: 30,199.5 sq miles (78,221 sq km)
Provinces: Albacete, Ciudad Real, Cuenca,
Guadalajara, Toledo.

9. Catalonia

Population: 5,958,208
Area: 12,327.5 sq miles (31,930 sq km)
Provinces: Barcelona, Gerona, Lerida,
Tarragona.

10. Extremadura

Population: 1,050,119
Area: 16,061.7 sq miles (41,602 sq km)
Provinces: Badajoz, Caceres.

11. Galicia

Population: 2,753,836
Area: 11,363.8 sq miles (29,434 sq km)
Provinces: La Coruna, Lugo, Orense,
Pontevedra

12. Madrid

Population: 4,726,986
Area: 3,086.7 sq miles (7,995 sq km)

13. Murcia

Population: 957,903
Area: 4,369.2 sq miles (11,317 sq km)

14. Navarre

Population: 507,367
Area: 4,023.3 sq miles (10,421 sq km)

15. Pais Vasco (Euzkadi)

Population: 2,134,967
Area: 2,803.3 sq miles (7,261 sq km)

16. Rioja

Population: 253,295
Area: 1,943.5 sq miles (5,034 sq km)

17. Valencia

Population: 3,646,765
Area: 8,997.6 sq miles (23,305 sq km)
Provinces: Alicante, Castellon, Valencia.

18. Ceuta and Melilla

Combined population: 129,313
Area: 12.3 sq miles (32 sq km)

Source: Cambio 16, Feb. 21, 1983.

"Rendition of Breda," by Diego Velásquez (1599–1660); Museo del Prado, Madrid.

"Las Meninas," by Velásquez; Museo del Prado, Madrid.

"View of Toledo," by Domenikos Theotocopoulos (El Greco) (1541–1614).

Santiago de Compostela (La Coruña).

Windmills in the Criptana country (Ciudad Real).

The Alhambra and Sierra Nevada, Granada.

Winter fair and ramparts, Ávila.

Francisco Franco and Manuel Benítez, 1965. The latter is the famous bullfighter "El Cordobés."

Plaza de las Cibeles, Madrid.

A beach in Galicia.

Fallas, La Plaza del Caudillo, Valencia. Fallas are the celebration on the eve of St. Joseph's Day (March 19). All the figures are burned in an enormous and dangerous bonfire.

April fair, Sevilla.

Plaza de Cataluña, Barcelona.

(Above) Entrance to the mausoleum, Valle de los Caídos (Valley of the Fallen), near Madrid. (Below) Roman bridge over the Guadiana, Mérida (Badajoz).

The cathedral of Santiago de Compostela, La Coruña.

Detail of the façade of La Mezquita (The Mosque), Córdoba.

Gothic City Hall in Barcelona: 14th–15th centuries.

Roman ramparts, Ávila.

Guell Park, Barcelona, the work of Gaudí.

El Escorial, royal monastery near Madrid.

Roman theater, Mérida.

Spanish stamps featuring Francisco Franco and King Juan Carlos.

Part 1

Roman Colony to Dictatorship

2

Conquest and Reconquest

The Iberian peninsula became part of the Roman Empire in 26 B.C. after two centuries of war. Rome fought first against the Carthaginians (the first and second Punic Wars, 264–241 B.C. and 218–201 B.C., the latter waged primarily in Spain) and then against the local peninsular peoples. Spain was unified for the first time under Rome, which created in the new colony a political and bureaucratic structure that endured for almost 400 years. Rome ruled through governors set up in the seven provinces into which the peninsula was eventually divided, creating new cities and expanding existing ones as centers for romanization where the various indigenous peoples were amalgamated into a single society.

Two devices were used to keep the Spaniards allegiant. Citizenship in a municipality, with its small-scaled imitation of imperial life in Rome, was rewarded with various inducements: reductions in tribute, grants of land, more efficient justice. For those with ambition and ability, the ultimate prize was life in Rome itself. Among Spanish talent that added glory to Rome were philosophers Marcus Seneca and his son Lucius; poet Lucan; epigramist Martial; geographer Pomponius Mela; Quintilian the orator, critic, and teacher; and the emperors Trajan, Hadrian, Marcus Aurelius, and Theodosius. Theodosius was the last emperor of the undivided empire, a convert to Christianity and the ruler who decreed what might be called the last legacy of Rome, one that took particularly strong root in Spain: religious orthodoxy. When Constantine converted from paganism to Christianity, he did so as an individual and did not compel the conversion of his subjects.

Theodosius, by contrast, used religion as a weapon of politics, and upon his conversion he decreed Christianity to be the official religion of the empire, thereby wedding church to state and equating heresy and treason.

As Theodosius had decreed, the empire was divided when he died. After A.D. 395 the eastern half was ruled from Constantinople, and the western half still governed from Rome. The reasons for this decision and for the decadence of the whole empire that had set in almost a century earlier is not germane to this study. What is important is that the weakness and corruption of Rome left all the component parts of the empire vulnerable, and by A.D. 409 the empire had collapsed in Spain.

INVASION FROM THE NORTH

Filling the vacuum left by the Romans, Suevians, Vandals, and Alans poured into the peninsula from northern Europe and quickly overpowered the natives. The cultural heritage of Rome withstood the barbarian onslaught in Spain, but the sociopolitical unity crumbled, leaving the Spaniards exposed to conquest. The centralism maintained by the emperors had seemingly never taken deep root in Spain, perhaps indicating the Spaniards' quarrelsome reluctance to be governed at all, and their preference, if being ruled were inevitable, for government as close to the people as possible. The first Germanic invaders were not successful in establishing their hegemony, however. They fought among themselves over the division of their conquests and were themselves conquered by the Visigoths, who moved into Spain in 414. By 475 the Visigoths had established total sovereignty, which they maintained for almost three centuries, governing from their capital, Toledo.

The influence of the Visigoths was far weaker than Roman influence, yet they left major legacies. The first was religion. The Visigoths who came to Spain were Arians, but savage opposition from the natives who had become Catholic under the empire persuaded the Visigothic king, Reccared, to convert to Catholicism in 587. Reccared declared his new faith to be the official religion of Spain, and for the second time, church and state were fused. The law, created by recasting diverse Visigothic and Hispano-Roman laws into a single code promulgated in 654, was the second legacy of the Visigoths. It fostered the reunification of Spanish society. The third legacy was the institution of the monarchy. The Roman unity of Spain had been based upon the sovereignty of the emperor in Rome whose will was made manifest through his agents, the governors. The Visigothic kings were the first to govern a unified Spain from *within* the country.

Succession to the Visigothic throne was not hereditary. It was the custom for the nobles to choose their king, yet this seemingly reasonable and democratic practice led to the demise of Visigothic rule and to the Muslim conquest of Spain. The moment a king died and the throne passed to his elected successor, the nobles who had been overlooked set out to contest the election. In 711, while King Roderic was away from Toledo putting down a Basque uprising, a disgruntled pretender conspired to replace him and, with the collusion of the bishop of Seville, sought the aid of the Arab governor of Morocco. The hierarchy of the Catholic church thus helped to expose Spain to the Muslim "infidel," and the ally who came to help unseat a king stayed to destroy the monarchy itself.

THE MUSLIM CONQUEST

The invaders who remained on the Iberian peninsula for almost eight centuries were not a single people. They are commonly called Arabs or Moors, but they also included Syrians, Berbers, and other races from North Africa and the Middle East. What unified all of these Semitic peoples was the Islamic faith they carried into Spain in 711, crossing at Gibraltar and spreading throughout the peninsula until they were stopped in 718 and pushed back by Christian forces led by the Visigothic nobleman Pelayo, at Covadonga in the mountains of Asturias. Theoretically, the Reconquest of Spain from the Moors began in that year, moving out of the isolated redoubts of Christianity left untouched by the Muslims in the cold and inhospitable north. However, the Reconquest proper did not begin until the eleventh century.

The Muslim conquests on the Iberian peninsula were unified into a single, dependent emirate of the caliphate in Damascus, until the ruling dynasty in Syria was overthrown in 750. Abd ar-Rahman I, a prince of the deposed Umayad family, fled to Spain and defeated the emir of Cordoba, who was governing in the name of the new caliph. Abd ar-Rahman I then proclaimed himself the monarch of the independent emirate of Al-Andalus, with its capital at Cordoba, and cut all ties with Damascus. It took almost two more centuries to consolidate the kingdom, however. The preeminence of Abd ar-Rahman and his descendants was challenged by local Muslim chieftains, who established small, independent kingdoms throughout the peninsula after 750. It was not until the reign of Abd ar-Rahman III (912–961) that the last vestiges of resistance to Cordoban rule were quashed and the independent emirate was converted into a caliphate equal in grandeur to that in Damascus.

The Cordoban emirate, and particularly the later caliphate, became the center of what many scholars consider to be one of the most brilliant civilizations (and undeniably the most exotic) ever to exist in western Europe. Following the division of the Roman Empire and the subsequent devastation of the Western Empire by the barbarians, scholarship and learning had gone into a deep decline in Christian Europe, but it was kept alive by Islamic scholars in the Middle East. Learning returned to Europe through Spain with the Arab invaders, who brought not only the knowledge of Greece and Rome but that of the Orient as well. The wonders of Muslim Spain attracted scholars and traders from throughout the Western world. Abd ar-Rahman III's private library is said to have contained 600,000 volumes, and he established over fifty public libraries throughout Al-Andalus. The study of jurisprudence, philosophy, grammar, mathematics, geometry, physics, astronomy, botany, music, architecture, medicine, and alchemy (the forerunner of chemistry) reached heights unprecedented in Europe. The decorative arts and landscape gardening were dazzling. Glass was invented in Cordoba in the ninth century, and paper (invented in Asia) was first brought into Europe through Spain. Moorish textiles, leather goods, and articles of precious metal were considered to be among the finest in the world. In agriculture, the Moors developed irrigation, perfected the huerta—which is still an integral part of Spanish farming—and are credited with introducing cotton, silk, sugar, rice, apricots, peaches, pomegranates, and oranges into Europe.

In 1011, after fifty years of misrule by the inept heirs of Abd ar-Rahman III, who died in 961, civil war broke out among the Muslim aristocracy of Al-Andalus. Twenty years later, the once powerful caliphate collapsed, and independent Islamic kingdoms called *taifas* emerged from its ruins.

THE RECONQUEST

In the 250 years following the battle at Covadonga, the Christians were able to push the Muslims no further back than a line along the Douro River that runs through the middle of the northwest quadrant of the Iberian peninsula. Below the Douro the Muslims were entrenched, and Christian advance had been stalled until Al-Andalus disintegrated in 1031, giving the Christians an advantage that they pursued relentlessly. The demise of Al-Andalus left Muslim Spain divided for conquest at a time when Christian Spain was sufficiently consolidated to pursue the religious crusade. By 1031 there were five Christian realms in Spain—Leon, Castile, Navarre, Aragon, and Catalonia, ruled by descendants of the warriors who had turned back the Muslims in 718. While slowly expanding Christian hegemony over the north of Spain, they contended among themselves, through battle and marriage, for political preeminence.

The Reconquest of Muslim Spain began in earnest in 1085, when Alfonso VI of Castile took Toledo from the Moors, leading an army made up of Castilians, Leonese, Galicians, Asturians, Basques, Navarrese, and Aragonese. Although these peoples were not yet united politically as Spaniards, they were already united spiritually as Catholics in their common hatred of Islam. For the next 200 years Christians and Muslims fought for the soul of Spain. In 1195 the Muslims crushed the Christians at the Battle of Alarcos and appeared to be in the ascendancy, but in 1212 the Christians defeated the Muslims in the single most important battle of the Reconquest at Navas de Tolosa. This marked the turning point in the Christian campaign against Islam. Never again were the Moors able to stop the Christians more than temporarily. Between 1236 and 1248 Cordoba, Jaén, Seville, and Murcia fell to the Castilians. In 1238 Valencia was taken by the Aragonese. By the end of the thirteenth century all of Spain was in the hands of Christian sovereigns with the exception of the taifa-kingdom of Granada.

By this time the Christian kingdoms had been reduced to three: Navarre, Aragon, and Castile. Catalonia became a part of Aragon through the first of the three great nuptial mergers that led to the unified Spanish nation-state. In 1137, the heir to the throne of Aragon married the sovereign of Catalonia, and their descendants ruled over the expanded kingdom of Aragon. In 1230, Castile and Leon were permanently united to form the kingdom of Castile, and in 1469, the last merger took place when Isabella, the heir to the throne of Castile, married Ferdinand, the heir to the throne of Aragon. By 1479, after Isabella and Ferdinand had ascended to their separate and independent thrones, only the kingdoms of Granada and Navarre kept the royal couple from ruling the entirety of Spain.[1] In 1481, the battle for Granada began. Eleven years later, on January 2, 1492—the single most important date in Spanish history— Ferdinand and Isabella victoriously accepted the keys to the city and its kingdom and expelled the last Muslim sovereign from Spain. After nearly 800 years, Spain was once again Catholic, and for their role in the final struggle between Christianity and Islam, Isabella and Ferdinand were from that time forward referred to as the Catholic Kings. Ferdinand conquered Navarre in 1512, eight years after the death of Isabella. Spain was then both Christian and united.

The unity of Spain obsessed the Catholic Kings, particularly Isabella, the Castilian, who saw her kingdom in the center of the country as the undisputed master of the peninsula. Even before Spain was united, Isabella and Ferdinand had begun to consolidate their authority by weakening the power of the great nobles who might have acted as a counterforce to their centralization. They enticed the grandees away from their estates to a life rich in favors and perquisites at the royal court. But the Catholic Kings did not touch the *fueros* (laws) or the *cortes*[2] (parliament) that continued to exist in the kingdoms that had been conjoined into the single nation-state. They sought to weaken these institutions, but they dared not dismantle them. Throughout the eight centuries of the Reconquest, the rulers of the Christian kingdoms had granted the fueros to entice and reward those warriors and their families willing to remain and colonize the isolated borderlands between Muslim and Christian domains. Once the battles had been won, the Christian kings returned to their headquarters to pursue dynastic ambitions against fellow Christian sovereigns, often not to return to the Reconquest for many years. Without permanent settlement and defense, newly won Chrisitan territories were vulnerable to reconquest by the Moors. The fueros granted political, commercial, and legal rights to those Christian pioneers willing to hazard the dangers of the frontier.

These fueros were cherished as immutable and perpetual and became an integral part of the sociopolitical fabric of Spanish life. A cortes was already functioning in both Castile and Aragon by the twelfth century and others were formed later in Leon, Catalonia, and Navarre. These bodies, made up of representatives from the nobles, the clergy, and the bourgeoisie, were summoned at the monarch's command when he or she needed more money than the royal coffers contained. The cortes would agree either to grant or withhold funds, always stressing its right to exist. The prerogative to have a voice in their own governance, whether in the fueros or the cortes, was a sentiment sacred to the Spaniards centuries before the emergence of modern democracy, and present-day separatism in post-Franco Spain has its origins in this tradition. These separate regional cortes continued to exist until the arrival of the Bourbons at the beginning of the eighteenth century, and remnants of the fueros persisted into the twentieth century. A single cortes representing the whole nation did not appear until the nineteenth century.

In the pursuit of unity, the Catholic Kings turned Catholicism to the service of the state. The separateness that was maintained through the fueros and the cortes would be overcome by religious solidarity and orthodoxy. The peoples of Spain, the vast majority of whom identified not with the new nation-state but with their regions, would become Spaniards through Catholicism, just as their ancestors had become reconquerors through the same faith. The singlemindedness of the pursuit of the Reconquest became the singlemindedness of the maintenance of the state. For the third time (the first was under the Romans, the second, under the Visigoths) church and state were wed, and treason and heresy once again became synonymous. With Isabella and Ferdinand, however, the fusion was accompanied by an intolerance that branded Spaniards with fanaticism. Ten years following the fall of Granada, the Catholic Kings reversed the terms of the treaty of surrender that had guaranteed freedom of religion to the Muslims in the defeated kingdom, a freedom reflective of the tolerance that had characterized life in both Christian and Muslim Spain for centuries.

From the very beginning of the Reconquest, Christians had lived in Muslim lands and Muslims in Christian lands, and Jews had lived in both. As frontiers between Muslim and Christian territories moved back and forth during the Reconquest, members of the three religions had oftentimes found themselves governed by men of other beliefs. If not with great love, they had lived together at least with respect and mutual acceptance. On February 11, 1502, that tolerance came to an end when the Catholic Kings decreed that all Muslims who would not convert to Catholicism would be expelled. Already on March 31, 1492, less than two months after the fall of Granada, Jews had been ordered either to be baptized as Catholics or to leave Spain within four months. Even earlier, in 1477, the new official religious intolerance with its political goals of national unity had been set in motion when the Catholic Kings established by decree what became known as the "New Inquisition," created primarily to examine *conversos,* Jews who had converted to Catholicism but whose fidelity to their new faith was suspect. The linkage between treachery and heresy had become fixed.

THE HAPSBURG DYNASTY: GLORY AND DECADENCE

With the death of the Catholic Kings, the German Hapsburgs came to rule Spain, heirs of the union between Juana, the daughter of Ferdinand and Isabella, and Philip, the son of Maximilian I, emperor of the Holy Roman Empire. When Isabella died in 1504 Juana inherited the crown of Castile, but when Ferdinand died in 1516 he left the crown of Aragon not to his daughter but to her son, Charles, for Juana had in the meantime been declared insane and locked away in a convent. After the death of his mother—who remained queen of Castile despite her madness and imprisonment—Charles became the first monarch since the time of the Visigoths to rule all of Spain from a single throne. Three years after he became King Charles I of Spain at the age of sixteen, he was elected Emperor Charles V of the Holy Roman Empire.

The reign of Charles V belongs more to the history of Europe than to the history of Spain. His realms included the Germanies and Austria (and parts of what would later be Czechoslovakia, Yugoslavia, and Poland); the Low Countries; parts of France (Franche Comté and Rousillon); over half of Italy; all of Spain; and all of the New World except Brazil (including a large part of what is today the United States). Charles was a visionary who dreamed on a global scale of a Europe politically united through his crown and spiritually united through Catholicism. Charles foresaw that Christian soldiers and missionaries bearing his banner would extend this unity to the New World.

As emperor, Charles had many enemies: Henry VIII of England, Francis I of France, Suleiman I of the Ottoman Empire, Pope Clement VII (in his temporal capacity as sovereign of Central Italy), and Martin Luther among them. He fought Francis and Henry for political supremacy and sacked Rome, taking Clement prisoner for failing to break an alliance with Francis. Charles fought the Turks who in the name of Muhammad were menacing the very gates of Vienna, and he struggled to crush Luther's ideas, which threatened the spiritual unity essential to his universalist scheme.

Charles's role as emperor transcended Spain, but his role as king is important for this overview. When Charles came to Spain to claim his throne in 1517 he had never before set foot in his country. He had been born and reared in the Low Countries and was Flemish in language and culture. He spoke no Spanish and was ignorant of Spanish mores, and he soon made a serious error in judgment, appointing a Fleming to act as regent when he left the country in 1520 to electioneer for the imperial crown. The people rose up in arms, not against the right of the king to rule but against his effrontery in ruling through a non-Spaniard. This was known as the revolt of the *comuneros*. Charles rectified his mistake and henceforth governed Spain by keeping the fueros intact and honoring the existence of the regional cortes. Unfortunately, Charles made incessant demands upon the legislatures to fund the pursuit of his worldwide ambitions, and he can be blamed for inflicting economic harm on Spain from which it suffered for generations. Yet he also thrust greatness on Spain, inaugurating its Golden Age; Charles took Spain with him, so to speak, into the enormous theater of the Holy Roman Empire. He forced upon Spaniards a cosmopolitanism that has ever since waged war in their souls against the provincialism that had its roots in the singular obsession of the Reconquest.

By 1555 Charles was exhausted, his dream of universal brotherhood and security unrealized. He was ahead of his time, an internationalist among nationalists, a believer in spiritual orthodoxy at a time when heterodoxy was rampant. He was a restless man whose dominions spanned continents but who had no home. Charles finally decided to give up his power, abdicating in Belgium in 1555. He retired to a remote spot in western Spain, the country that he had grown to love but that he had not visited in thirteen years when he returned. When he abandoned his thrones he divided his domains and gave the Hapsburg Empire to his brother Ferdinand. To his son Philip, he gave Spain, the New World, the Italian possessions, and the Low Countries. Charles died in 1558.

Philip II was the first *Spaniard* on the throne; he was not a Fleming like Charles nor a Castilian like Isabella nor an Aragonese like Ferdinand. He possessed characteristics and values that Spaniards came to honor: an almost mystical devotion to Spain and to Spanish unity, a dedication to the work of being king, and a profound religious faith. Philip ruled with the fueros and the regional cortes relatively untouched, as had his father, but he acted to centralize the state administratively and symbolically by creating a permanent capital in 1561. Until Philip II chose Madrid, an obscure Castilian village in the geographic center of the peninsula, as the capital, the government had been located wherever the monarchs happened to be as they crisscrossed their realms in constant travel.

Philip pursued political unity relentlessly through religious orthodoxy. The cruel alternatives presented to the Moors by the Catholic Kings—renounce Islam or leave Spain—had produced converts in name only who resisted absorption into the Christian life. Sixty years later they were still steeped in the Islamic culture and faith; moreover, they were thought to be in close contact with Turkish coreligionists whose control of the Mediterranean Charles V had been unable to break and who continued to threaten the Christian hegemony of Europe. In 1568 the Muslim converts in Alpujarra, a village in the province of Granada, revolted against the king. Philip put his troops under the command of his half-brother Don Juan of Austria, and after two years of savage fighting, with atrocities committed by both Christians and Muslims, the revolt was put down and the Granadan Arabs were scattered like so much debris throughout Spain. The following year Don Juan crushed the Turkish sea power at the naval battle of Lepanto, off the coast of Greece, accomplishing for the rest of the continent what his great-grandparents had accomplished for Spain: the eradication of what Christians in that militant religious age saw as the scourge of Islam.

Philip II did not achieve a comparable triumph over Protestantism, which he considered to be no less heinous than Islam. In the Low Countries (particularly in the United Provinces, later called the Netherlands), Protestantism had made deep inroads not only as a religious force undermining the papacy but as a political force undermining Spain. For the Dutch, to be Protestant was to be anti-Spanish, and to be anti-Spanish was to support independence. In 1579 the Netherlands declared its independence with the help of England. Protestantism linked the two nations spiritually, but England had more than religion to inspire her. In the struggle for political supremacy in Europe and in the colonies, Spain was England's most formidable opponent. Anything that weakened Spain strengthened England, and the revolt of the Dutch undermined Spanish power. Elizabeth I of England relished Spain's predicament and did everything possible to exacerbate it. Philip took up the challenge for Spain and for Catholicism, and launched the Spanish Armada in 1588 to humble England, crush its sea power, and cut its lifelines. His defeat was psychologically devastating. Although Spain emerged from the disaster still a great nation, hindsight now tells us that 1588 represented the zenith of Spanish power in the world.

Our account of Spanish political history accelerates significantly after the death of Philip II in 1598. The main themes of politics had already been established by that date: unity and separatism; regional rights (the fueros and the cortes); religious orthodoxy; and the unity of church and state with its equation of heresy and treason. These themes endured for generations, even centuries, and most of them are still present in modern Spain. Philip II was followed by successors unworthy of their heritage, and during the reigns of the last Hapsburgs—Philip III, Philip IV, and Charles II—the degeneration of Spain paralleled the degeneration of the sovereigns themselves. Internationally, the final humiliation came in 1643 at the Battle of Rocroi in the rebellious Low Countries, when French troops routed Spain's most celebrated soldiers, the Tercios. Spain thus suffered defeat by both England and

France, the two nations that eclipsed Spain to become the major European powers for the next 250 years.

Spain continued to be an integral part of the European scene, but played only a secondary role after the 1600s. Domestically, Spain continued its self-mutilation. In 1609, the Spanish expelled all Moors from the national territory, casting out a people who had lived on the peninsula for nearly 900 years. With the Jews gone since 1492 and the Moors banished, Spain had crippled itself. The Moors and the Jews had been among the most creative people in Spanish history, and when they were driven out, their genius went unreplaced.

NOTES

1. The royal motto of Isabella and Ferdinand symbolized their separateness within their unity, or more precisely the separate entity of each sovereign's realm within the unity of Spain created by the sovereigns' marriage. The motto has almost become symbolic of the separateness within unity of the peoples of Spain even today. *Tanto Monta Monta Tanto Isabel Como Fernando.* The motto is difficult to translate smoothly and succinctly. Awkwardly but accurately translated it says: "Isabella mounts the throne with sovereignty equal to that of Ferdinand who mounts the throne with sovereignty equal to that of Isabella."

2. The word *cortes* is both singular and plural.

3

Spain Under the Bourbons

Charles II produced no heirs, and when he died his throne went to the French Duke of Anjou, Philip, grandson of Louis XIV and Maria Theresa, Charles's sister. The legacy was challenged by the English, who feared that France would become the master of Europe if there were Bourbon kings on both sides of the Pyrenees. Never was it more clear that Spain had ceased to be a major nation and had become the pawn of more powerful ones. The choice of Spain's next sovereign was decided by the War of the Spanish Succession, in which England allied with Portugal, the Netherlands, and the Holy Roman Empire to support the Hapsburg archduke, Charles, against France and a hapless Spain. France was victorious, and the French duke became Philip V, the first Bourbon on the Spanish throne.

Like the Hapsburgs before them, the Spanish Bourbons involved Spain in European dynastic intrigues and wars that continued to drain the country's dwindling resources with little benefit to Spain. On the contrary, Spain lost colonies bartered in treaties that secured peace only temporarily. Spain fought wars with France, England, and the Holy Roman Empire in 1719; with England in 1739; with the Holy Roman Empire in 1740; with England again in 1762; with Portugal (in Brazil) in 1776; and for a fourth time with England (the American Revolution) in 1779.

Domestically, the Spanish Bourbons reversed the policies of the Hapsburgs and their predecessors, enforcing political unity by destroying almost all the fueros and the regional cortes. These traditional institutions meant nothing to the newly arrived Bourbons, who patterned their centralist policies after Louis XIV, who allowed no political institutions to stand between the sovereign and his subjects. Philip V stripped Catalonia, Aragon, and Valencia of their historic rights and representative bodies. He was particularly vengeful against these provinces because they had supported the Hapsburg pretender in the War of the Spanish Succession, but the king was only slightly less severe with the Basque provinces and Navarre, which had used better judgment. Philip made it clear that the Bourbons would tolerate no enfringement on the absolutism of the king or on the authority of the center. Philip's policy seriously undermined the legitimacy of the Bourbon house among its new subjects, and not until the reign of Charles III (1759–1788), one of Spain's few good rulers, were the Bourbons accepted as legitimate sovereigns and legitimate Spaniards, despite their French origins and their flouting of Spanish traditions.

THE NAPOLEONIC INTERLUDE

The people's loyalty was tested during the reign of the two kings who succeeded Charles III—Charles IV and Ferdinand VII, the two worst sovereigns in Spanish history. Ferdinand was perhaps the worst of all. Their reigns are important because they are part of the Napoleonic history of Spain. In 1808, Charles IV was deposed by Napoleon and replaced by the latter's brother, Joseph Bonaparte. The people of Madrid responded to this usurpation by revolting against the French occupiers on May 2, 1808, and the uprising spread throughout the country. The War of Independence—as Spaniards call this guerrilla war—lasted from 1808 to 1814, when the Spanish finally ousted the French. The Peninsular War— as it is called by non-Spaniards—was part of the larger European campaign against Napoleon, and victory over the French came primarily because of British intervention in Spain. The valor of the Spanish people cannot be denied, however. Ironically, they fought in the name of Ferdinand VII, whose father had been far more despotic (and corrupt and inefficient) than Joseph Bonaparte, who had brought a constitution that in many ways was quite progressive. The Spaniards fought for what they considered to be the legitimate Spanish royal house, and they mythologized Ferdinand VII, the heir of the deposed Charles IV, as *el deseado*, the desired one, who would bring honor back to Spain.

During the hiatus of authority that lasted while the Bourbons were out of Spain and the Napoleonic rulers were fighting to maintain their control, self-governing juntas sprang up throughout the country. These juntas elected representatives to an assembly that met from 1809 to 1813 in Cádiz on the South Atlantic coast, out of French reach. This was the first cortes in Spanish history representing all of the country in a single legislative body. From this cortes came the celebrated liberal constitution of 1812 that established the terms of the Bourbon restoration: a limited monarchy with separation of powers; full guarantee of civil and human rights; land reform for uncultivated acreage; abolition of all existing seignorial rights; local self-government; abolition of slavery; public education; and tax reform. The constitution recognized Catholicism as the state religion, but it abolished the Inquisition, restricted the number of monasteries and convents, and required the clergy to pay taxes.

Ferdinand VII repudiated the entire constitution the moment he ascended the throne in 1814, and reestablished a regime more absolutist than that of Charles IV. Ferdinand's repression became so severe that the people revolted in 1820, reestablished a constitutional monarchy, and in an action that defies logic, requested the same Ferdinand to return as king. Ferdinand swore fidelity to the constitution, but after his reactionary French cousin Charles X sent troops to restore absolutism to Spain, Ferdinand once again showed his true colors, reverting to the despotism that had characterized his earlier behavior.

POLITICAL DEVELOPMENTS

The reaction to the constitution of 1812 and to the reign of Ferdinand VII shaped political alignments for the remainder of the nineteenth century. Yet just as during the War of

Independence, when long-suffering patriots fought in the name of the despotic Bourbon house, the philosophical positions after 1814 were not neat. The Liberals accepted the constitution, the limited government, and the guarantees of civil rights, but they rejected the historic regional rights that antedated the constitution. They would tolerate no restrictions on the absolute sovereignty of the central government, and were determined to weaken the power of the church by confiscating its property. The Conservatives rejected the constitution, supported an autocratic monarchy and a militant church, repudiated the guarantees of civil and political rights set forth in the document, but championed the ancient democratic fueros that the Bourbons had all but destroyed.

When Ferdinand died in 1833 without a male heir, his throne passed to his daughter, Isabella, who was still a child. Under the Bourbon Salic law a female could not inherit the crown; under the tradition of the Hapsburgs and under the even older traditions that preceded them, a woman could inherit. The Liberals supported Isabella; the Conservatives rejected her and in the name of Ferdinand's brother, Charles, began a civil war fought primarily in the Basque country, Navarre, and Catalonia. The war continued until 1839. In the meantime, Spain was ruled by the regents of Isabella, first her mother and then, following the mother's exile, General Espartero. After 1843 the queen herself ascended the throne, but her reign became so corrupt and morally scandalous (her amorous life was the talk of Europe) that she was forced to abdicate after a revolution in 1868.

From the viewpoint of future Spanish politics, the most far-reaching event of Isabella's reign was the confiscation of church property, which took place during the administration of Liberal prime minister Juan Álvarez Mendizábal.[1] The church lost most of its independence of action when it lost its sources of revenue. Henceforth, the state paid the salaries of its clergymen under the terms of the concordat negotiated with the Vatican in 1851. Its dependence on the state turned the Spanish church into the state's apologist, a posture that reached its ultimate development during the Franco regime. True enough, there had been an intimate relationship between church and state since the Reconquest, but it had been a relationship between equals, not between subventioner and supplicant.

After the revolution, the military again ruled Spain until a new king was chosen in 1870. The selection of Amadeo, the brother of King Victor Emmanuel II of Italy, prompted the Carlists to rise again, and another civil war ensued. This time the Republicans, a new force in Spanish politics, joined the Carlists in opposing the king, and in 1873 the hapless Amadeo abdicated. A republic was established that lasted less than a year. During this time it had four presidents and was constantly at war with the Carlists. Finally, the insurgents were subdued, and as punishment for the Carlists' challenge to national unity, Madrid abolished all remaining fueros except a few minor ones allowed to Navarre.

The Bourbons were restored in 1875 in the person of King Alfonso XII, Isabella's son, who ruled with extensive power under a new constitution created in 1876. The cabinet was responsible to the king and not to the bicameral legislature that could be summoned, prorogued, and dismissed by the monarch. The monarch's only restriction was that the legislature be replaced within three months of dismissal. Alfonso had the makings of a good sovereign, but unfortunately, he died young. Alfonso was succeeded by his queen, Maria Cristina, who was pregnant with the heir born King Alfonso XIII in 1886. The queen acted as regent until 1902, when the king reached the age of sixteen and ascended the throne with full power.

THE SECOND RESTORATION

Several issues of major importance for later Spanish politics have their origins during the decades of misrule between the Bourbon restoration in 1814 and the second restoration of 1875, a period that included thirty-five military uprisings, or *pronunciamientos*,[2] eleven considered successful. First, the military entered the political arena, where it would remain a formidable presence until the end of the Franco regime, and even into the post-Franco era. Second, regionalism took on a new dimension as Catalonia and the Basque country (the two centers of dissidence before the restoration in 1875) became the country's most prosperous regions. The people of both areas believed that the government in Madrid drained them financially through taxation without granting them commensurate political power in return. Catalonia was particularly incensed, for it had become the manufacturing center of the nation, and wanted tariffs to protect its new industries. Catalonia, along with the Basque provinces, demanded the return of regional rights, the fueros, that would give them a degree of political and economic freedom and flexibility. Third, socialism gave an increasingly strident voice to the growing proletariat of Catalonia, the Basque provinces, and Asturias, the coal mining center of Spain. Equally shrill was the anarchist voice of discontent, heard both in rural Andalucia and in urban Catalonia.

During the regency of Maria Cristina, these issues fermented while Spain enjoyed a rare period of relatively stable government. Once the second uprising of the Carlists had been put down in 1875, the oligarchy, although divided politically into the Liberal and Conservative parties, realized that only solidarity against the increasingly urgent demands of the masses could preserve the kind of Spain enjoyed by the gentry. Antonio Cánovas del Castillo and Práxedes Sagasta, leaders of the Conservative and Liberal parties, arrived at a tacit agreement to put aside past differences and to govern Spain in rotation, securing the necessary electoral majorities by rigging national elections, which under the constitution of 1876 guaranteed universal male suffrage. The two major party chiefs then worked to forestall further revolt among the Carlists by offering to make the movement's defeated military commanders officers in the armed forces of the restored monarchy. Given the pandemonium of Spanish politics between the first restoration of the Bourbons in 1814 and the second in 1875, some believe that the peace and order achieved by the Liberal-Conservative collusion was worth the price of constitutional corruption. An additional price was paid, however, that boded ill for long-term peace and order. The trade-off between the two elite parties froze a socioeconomic status quo that excluded both the growing urban proletariat of Catalonia and the Basque lands, whose frustration was mounting, and the Andalucian peasantry, whose requests for land reform were rapidly becoming demands. Forced out of meaningful politics and deprived of effective electoral expression, the lower classes turned to socialism and anarchism. Eventually, they also turned to direct action: strikes, violence, and assassination.

The death of Cánovas in 1897, the assassination of Sagasta in 1903, and the accession of the boy-king Alfonso XIII in 1902 put an end to the artificial stability. The two major parties fractionalized as they searched for new leadership, and the growing social and regional unrest generated a proliferation of new parties. The lack of clear legislative majorities played into the hands of the new king, who manipulated unstable coalitions to his advantage. Alfonso lacked both political intelligence and scruples, and he had grandiose notions of kingly rights that, irrespective of their constitutionality, were out of step with the political realities of the twentieth century. Moreover, he took his title of commander-in-chief of the armed forces literally, giving the military his tacit approval to act without informing the Cortes.

During Alfonso's reign proletarian disquiet continued to mount, particularly in Catalonia. In 1909, during what was later called *la semana trágica* (the tragic week) the masses took to the streets in Barcelona in an outburst of class hatred hitherto unknown in Spain, unleashed against all the forces of oppression—military, political, and economic. Gerald Brenan described the event as "five days of mob rule in which union leaders lost all control of their men, and twenty-two churches and thirty-four convents were burned. Monks were killed, tombstones were desecrated and strange and macabre scenes took place as when workers danced in the streets with the disinterred mummies of nuns."[3]

Frightened as never before, the oligarchy retaliated by organizing private police forces, often made up of little more than paid killers. The violence between these toughs and the ruffians of the Socialist labor union (Unión General de Trabajadores, General Workers' Union) and the Anarchist trade union (Confederación Nacional de Trabajadores, National Workers' Confederation) accelerated year by year. Between 1917 and 1921, there were 1,472 political crimes committed in the major cities of Spain, 809 in Barcelona alone.[4] Unfortunately for the solidarity of the workers, the violence between socialists and anarchists was often as bloody as between the labor groups and the hired gunmen of the oligarchy.

The intensification of proletarian fury led to a change in the political orientation of the Basque and Catalan socio-economic elites, particularly the latter. The "stalemate society" achieved by Cánovas and Sagasta had maintained the preindustrial and precapitalist values favored by the majority of the Spanish gentry—the landowners, ranchers, citrus and olive growers, the mine owners and operators. The burgeoning capitalist entreprenurial class of Catalonia and the Basque territories suffered from discrimination by the political decision makers in Madrid, who maintained a policy of free trade beneficial to producers of raw materials and foodstuffs meant for export. The Catalans and Basques wanted protection for infant industries and chafed under Madrid's restrictions. Their demands for autonomy were as much economic in origin as cultural or historical. The desire to escape what was considered centrist suffocation grew stronger, yet the behavior of the workers eventually caused the regional oligarchy to fear the proletariat more than it hated the government in Madrid, which commanded the forces of law and order indispensable to crush labor violence. Catalonia muted its clamor for autonomy in exchange for protection from Madrid, and by royal decree Alfonso rewarded the region with a partial restoration of fueros in the form of a highly symbolic but almost powerless legislative body called the Mancomunidad.

THE ROLE OF THE MILITARY

Catalonia's new political posture played into the hands of the armed forces, whose arrogance had been growing since the turn of the century. The military had come to consider itself indispensable to public order and immune to civilian political control. It excoriated any individual or group whose behavior, in its opinion, undermined national unity—not only the socialist and the anarchist lower classes but the regionalist upper classes as well.

The military first entered domestic politics when most of the overseas army returned to Spain after the Latin American colonies (with the exception of Cuba and Puerto Rico) declared themselves independent during the reign of Joseph Bonaparte. The remaining colonial forces returned after their humiliating defeat in the Spanish-American War of 1898. Back for good, the military sought a place to redeem its honor, and decided upon Morocco. The cities of Ceuta and Melilla on the Moroccan coast had been Spanish for centuries—Melilla since 1497, Ceuta since 1581. After the turn of the twentieth century, when the European powers were jockeying to occupy what still remained native on the African continent, the Spanish military set out to annex the hinterland of the two Spanish cities, with the sanction of Alfonso XIII. The resistance put up by the local Berber tribes was as fierce as it was unexpected, and the Spanish soldiers—mostly recruits from the poorer classes that could not afford to buy off the military service of their sons—were literally slaughtered, 10,000 in one battle alone at Anual.

The reaction at home was volcanic. The Cortes began an investigation of the army and of the king's alleged collusion, but before its report could be made General Miguel Primo de Rivera executed a coup d'état in 1923 that abolished the constitution. Primo proclaimed himself dictator, and Alfonso XIII remained as the figurehead of state, an arrangement that suited both the king and the caudillo. Without Primo, the king would probably have lost his throne; without Alfonso, the dictator would have lacked legitimacy.

THE LAST DECADE OF BOURBON RULE

At the beginning, the dictatorship was far from universally condemned. The working class, the small middle class, and the intelligentsia suffered from Primo's rigid censorship and his abolition of free trade unions and political parties. The classes that ran Spain, however—primarily the landowners but also the new industrialists—were satisfied with the general's accomplishments and welcomed the protection that the army afforded against domestic violence and strikes. To Primo's credit, he initiated improvements such as highway and railway construction and hydroelectric and irrigation projects. Unfortunately, his ambitions overreached Spain's resources, and when the post–World War I boom slid toward the depression of the late 1920s, Spain found itself seriously overextended economically. Spectacular events such as the world fairs held in Seville and Barcelona were insufficient to stimulate the lagging economy or regenerate a destitute part of the country like Andalucia. Primo's failure to solve the economic crisis dampened the support of earlier enthusiasts, and his bad judgment in other areas contributed to his waning popularity. He courted the church, but his strategy backfired. Primo failed in his attempt to extend to a private Jesuit and a private Augustinian college the right to grant official university degrees, a privilege traditionally enjoyed exclusively by the state universities. His orders to revoke the Mancomunidad granted by Alfonso alienated most of the Catalan elite who had earlier been his champions.

As long as the army stayed loyal, there was little anyone could do to remove Primo, though the king was also becoming increasingly restive in his figurehead role. Primo then made a fatal mistake. In his rush to reform Spain and to cut expenses, he decided to reduce the gargantuan officer corps. At the time, the ratio of officers to soldiers in the Spanish military was the highest in Europe. The army elite immediately appealed to Alfonso to countermand Primo's orders, switching allegiance from the dictator to the king. With the army on his side, Alfonso demanded Primo's resignation, eager to cleanse himself of the caudillo's contamination. The general was in no position to bargain, and chose to resign. In January 1930 he left for France, where he died a few months later.

Primo's resignation came too late to save either the monarch or the monarchy. Opposition to the crown had developed even within impeccably conservative groups for whom republicanism had previously been synonymous with revolution. Alfonso tried to hold on, appointing a civilian government to replace Primo, but he would not call elections. The king was faced with a dilemma. If it were judged that the dictatorship had merely interrupted constitutional continuity, then the 1876 constitution was still in force and elections had to be called. If the dictatorship had destroyed the constitution, then a new one had to be created by an elected constituent assembly either to restore the monarchy or establish a republic. If elections were not called and Alfonso chose to remain, he would become a dictator and thereby destroy the honor of the Bourbon royal house.

Alfonso opted for three successive elections: municipal, provincial, and parliamentary. He hoped that antimonarchical sentiments would cool by the time the parliamentary elections were held, but the results of the municipal elections were so overwhelmingly prorepublican in the big cities and in all the provincial capitals except Cádiz that the king decided upon voluntary exile. His move was perhaps prompted by the action of the city councils of Oviedo, Seville, and Valencia in proclaiming the Republic of Spain and by the action of the Catalan separatists, who deliriously (and prematurely) announced the Republic of Catalonia. Even the commander of the civil guard, General José Sanjurjo, declared for the republic. The army had already disassociated itself from the king, who was left alone and powerless. On April 14, 1931, Alfonso left Spain, never to return. He did not abdicate, however; he simply went into exile in Rome, where he died in 1949.

NOTES

1. The liberal state did not give the lands of the church to the poor. Liberalism in Spain was much like liberalism throughout the rest of Europe—a burgeois phenomenon supported by a class that hated and feared the poor and the dispossessed as much as conservatives did. The Liberals sought not to eliminate the Conservatives as a class but only their antique, precapitalist political and economic privileges. Consequently the lands were sold to those who could afford to pay for them, not only the new liberal bourgeoisie but also the old conservative artistocracy. Greed to

acquire more land lured the traditional elites (who were devout Catholics) to swallow their repugnance for the Liberals, who had so generously provided their windfall, and to embrace the hated liberal state. Liberals and Conservatives would cooperate again after the second Bourbon restoration in 1875.

2. The historian Vicens Vives defines *pronunciamiento* as a military uprising usually consisting merely of subverting all or part of the army and sometimes the police force, thereby depriving the government of the means to defend itself. See Vicens Vives, *Approaches to the History of Spain,* trans. and ed. Joan Connelly Ullmann (Berkeley: University of California Press, 1967).

3. Gerald Brenan, *The Spanish Labyrinth* (New York: Macmillan, 1944), p. 34.

4. Stanley G. Payne, *The Spanish Revolution* (New York: W. W. Norton, 1970), p. 60.

4

Democracy and Civil War

THE SECOND REPUBLIC

By 1931, the republic was an idea whose time had come. The monarchy had ended ignominiously after the collapse of the dictatorship, and the prestige of the army, which had propped up both institutions, had fallen precipitously after both masters were repudiated. When the time for the republic finally arrived, however, the great majority of Spaniards were unable to perform the difficult and self-disciplined task of making democracy work. Much like Germany prior to the Weimar Republic, Spain prior to the Second Republic lacked democratic experience. The democracy of republican politics existed in isolation within a nondemocratic society. The family, the church, the schools, the bureaucracy, the workplace, the trade unions, the political parties (including those on the Left) were autocratic organizations that afforded the Spaniard little opportunity to learn how to play the democratic game. In short, the political system was incongruent with the socio-economic system, to use Harry Eckstein's analysis.[1]

The electoral system devised for the Second Republic exacerbated an already unrealistic political system. Designed to produce stability and to reward the strongest parties, the electoral system gave an exaggerated majority to the victors at the polls. The party or coalition of parties that won a majority, no matter how slight (51 to 49 percent, for example), received a disproportionately large number of legislative seats. For example, the winning party or coalition in Madrid would receive 13 out of the city's 17 seats in the Cortes; in Barcelona, the winner would take 16 of the 20 seats.

The first artificial legislative majority went to the Left, inaugurating what is now referred to as the Red Biennium (December 9, 1931, to December 31, 1933). In fact, the domination of the Left began with the elections to the constituent assembly that became the first legislature of the new republic following the approval of the constitution by the Cortes. The leftists in power included the Liberals, who in accordance with the European liberal tradition were liberal on civil and political rights, but conservative on economic issues. Only a part of the Left was Marxist, but on questions of church and state the Liberals matched the Marxists in their deep anti-Catholic prejudice, and this position was clearly spelled out in the controversial constitution approved by the Cortes in 1931.

The Constitution of 1931

Instead of a balanced, objective instrument designed to accommodate the nation as a whole, the constitution of 1931 can best be described as a weapon to humble the Right. This is particularly true of the articles regarding religion. The church had indeed become a corrupt institution, pandering since the middle of the nineteenth century to the wealthy classes, and it probably deserved its constitutional comeuppance. Realistically, however, the emotionally charged articles on religion could only enflame what was still a strongly Catholic nation. Devout Catholics could not fail to condemn a constitution whose articles declared freedom of religion; abolished the state clerical budget; closed all Catholic schools except seminaries (in a country in which over half of all schools were Catholic); forbade all clergy to teach in state schools; outlawed the Jesuits and confiscated their property; legalized divorce; and abolished religious burial unless specifically provided for by the deceased. None of the economic provisions—on land reform, for example—inspired nearly the antirepublican sentiment that the gratuitously anticlerical and antireligious articles did. Furthermore, most of Spain's very large and influential clerical population were far from wealthy; the average parish priest, for example, lived on an income little different from his parishioners. The church's wealth, which had gradually been rebuilt since the confiscations of the mid-1800s, was enjoyed only by the ecclesiastical elite. To cut off a humble priest's meager pay and then prevent him from earning a living in the state schools was to create a body of antirepublican zealots. These opponents could have been supporters of the socioeconomic reforms of the Left had they been handled more logically and less emotionally by the framers of the constitution.

The Right was determined to undo the entire document, and it got the chance with the elections that ushered in the "Black Biennium" (December 31, 1933, to February 16, 1936). Leftists claimed that the victory of the Right was due in part to the support of the newly enfranchised women voting on instruction from their priests. The Right also won because the anarchists deprived the Left of enormous electoral support by refusing to go to the polls, which would have compromised their antistatist ideology. Like the leftist government that preceded it, the rightist government reflected an artificial majority in the Cortes, and it behaved as blindly and as unintelligently, politically speaking, as had the Left from 1931 to 1933.

The Struggle Between Left and Right

When the Right began to reverse the laws passed by the Left and to amend the constitution, the Left in the Cortes— as represented by Manuel Azaña, the prime minister during the Red Biennium and the motive force during the constituent assembly—announced that it was breaking all association with the existing institutions of the country. Nothing could be more indicative of the Spaniard's absolute incomprehension of the spirit of democratic politics than this outburst from Azaña, who was effectively saying that if the institutions of the state were used to produce legislation that he and his followers disliked, then the institutions would be ignored. Yet Azaña had helped create these very institutions and had used them in precisely the same way during the preceding two years. The rightist government then matched the political ignorance of the Left by pardoning General José Sanjurjo, who had attempted a coup d'état during the Red Biennium. The Right was effectively taking the position that a conspiracy to overthrow the government was acceptable as long as the government in power was leftist.

By autumn of 1934, the tension between the Right and the Left outside the parliament exceeded that inside the parliament, and it finally broke when the working classes rose up in Madrid, Barcelona, and Oviedo. The revolts in Madrid and Barcelona were quickly put down, but the rebellion in Asturias, which involved over 30,000 workers, raged for almost two weeks before being crushed by the army. Eminent American historian Stanley Payne, a man not given to exaggeration, has called this uprising the most intensive, destructive proletarian insurrection in the history of western Europe to that date.[2] The even more eminent Spanish historian, Salvador de Madariaga, a moderate conservative, has written: "With the rebellion of 1934 the Left lost every shred of moral authority to condemn the rebellion of 1936."[3]

However one views the events of 1934, it was clear from that time forward that there would be no peaceful solution to Spain's Left-Right conflict. City streeets and country roads became scenes of battle among paramilitary organizations reflecting the entire political spectrum, and the official forces of order—the army, the Civil Guard, the Frontier Customs Guards, and the newly created Assault Guards—were themselves divided ideologically. Most supported the Right; some supported the Left. The elections held in February 1936 returned political control to the Left, but once again the electoral system produced an artificial majority as inconclusive as that of 1931 or 1933, thus failing to resolve the dilemma politically.

The new government, called the Popular Front, was a fragile alliance of leftist parties, including the Communists. Its program, less extreme than that of 1931, could be considered more social democratic than socialist, and the anticlerical obsession had abated. Yet deep divisions among the leftist parties prevented the government from implementing its reforms and doomed the Second Republic to a precipitous sweep to the Left inside the Cortes and insurgence by the Right outside. Blame must fall particularly hard on the Socialist party, the largest party in the Popular Front, which was rent by conflict between the increasingly revolutionary and rigidly orthodox Francisco Largo Caballero and the more moderate Indalecio Prieto. De Madariaga has stated flatly: "What made the Spanish Civil War inevitable was the Civil War within the Socialist party."[4]

What ultimately triggered the Spanish Civil War was the government's pardon of the insurgents in 1934. The government had obviously learned nothing from Sanjurjo's pardon two years earlier. The paramilitary forces of the Right reacted to the government's flagrantly provocative behavior with street violence, matched by violence from the paramilitary forces of the Left. On July 12, right-wing parliamentary leader José Calvo Sotelo was taken from his home and murdered by the prorepublican Assault Guards, in retaliation for the killing of one of the guard's officers by three antirepublican Falangists that same day. On July 17, 1936, the military finally rose up against the government from its camps in Morocco, and the next morning the rebellion spread to Spain. Within days the rebellion turned into a civil war that was to last three years.

CIVIL WAR

The Spanish Civil War was first and foremost *Spanish,* irrespective of the involvement of other nations that either aided the republicans (called the Loyalists) or the insurgents or rebels (called the Nationalists), or refused to aid either. The democracies, especially Great Britain, France, and the United States, refused to help their kindred democracy, though Spain deserved assistance under the rules of international law. Germany and Italy supported the rebels with arms, munitions, personnel, and money, and after the democracies turned their backs the Soviet Union provided aid to the republic, which cost it very dearly. The story of the interplay of international forces has been told and retold, yet the recounting often seems to diminish the Spanishness of the war. This is particularly true when the war is seen as a prelude to World War II, which broke out five months after the end of the war in Spain. In the Second World War, Germany and Italy again fought the Soviet Union, just as they had in Spain, but this time, the democracies fought in league with the Communists. All these international convolutions notwithstanding, the war in Spain was Spanish in origin, pursuit, and outcome, and though the ending might have been different if the foreign involvement had been different, the Spanish Civil War would have occurred even if the rest of the world had done nothing but watch.

The Republican Camp

The uprising of the generals in Morocco precipitated not only the Civil War between the Loyalists and the Nationalists but also a civil war among the Loyalists, deeply divided into what de Madariaga called "a true revolutionary hydra with a Syndicalist, an Anarchist, two Communist, and three Socialist heads, furiously biting at each other."[5] The major Socialist party, the Spanish Socialist Worker's Party, was split into two factions, the moderate half headed by Prieto, the extreme by Largo Caballero. The third Socialist head was the Unified Socialist Party of Catalonia. The Communists were divided between the main national party and its Catalan counterpart. There was yet another head not mentioned by de Madariaga— the dissident Marxist, anti-Stalinist, Trotskyite party, the Workers' Party of Marxist Unification. Much of the energy the Loyalists should have directed against the insurgents was spent instead among fellow republicans, seeking to remake Spain in the image of each group's ideology. At issue in this civil war within the Loyalist camp was the question of priorities. Which should be pursued first—the larger or the smaller civil war? Should all efforts be exerted to defeat the insurgents, delaying the revolution until the war was won, or should the revolution be carried on simultaneously within the larger Civil War, and given precedence if necessary?

The extremists, particularly the syndicalists and the anarchists, fervently believed that the revolution should be pursued while the larger war raged. The less radical elements, the liberals and the moderate socialists, felt equally strongly that the larger war should be won first. Socioeconomic reform would then come in its wake. The Communist party joined the more moderate voices, and as a result was branded as counterrevolutionary by the militant socialists and anarchists. During the early months of the Civil War, the Communist party appeared to represent stability and caution. Raymond Carr wrote:

> The Jacobin paradox—that a party whose revolutionary credentials and ultimate revolutionary intentions are above reproach is best equipped to risk a policy of temporary social conservation—brought the Communist party a flood of recruits. Its membership rose from perhaps 40,000 in July, 1936, to 250,000 by March, 1937, and in the process it almost ceased to be a workers' party.[6]

The Spanish Communists had suddenly muted their revolutionary voice following directions from the leaders in Moscow who reasoned that the defeat of the republic would turn Spain if not into an ally of Germany and Italy then at least into a supporter of their anti-Communist policy. A republican victory, on the other hand, would have come about primarily because of Soviet aid. Postwar Spain could then be communized automatically without need for the revolution, and the Soviet Union should have a totally dependent ally in Western Europe.

In the immediate aftermath of the insurrection, republican Spain fragmented into self-governing juntas, defended by militias loyal primarily to their own ideology—whether communist, socialist, anarchist, or syndicalist. There were few governmental orders from Madrid, which was under siege and cut off from much of the country, and for all practical purposes, there was no republican army. The overwhelming majority of the national armed forces had defected to the insurgents. The republic was bravely defended by the various militias, but each fought as it saw fit in the name of its own belief. There was no overall republican command or direction.

The advisers from the USSR, who accompanied Soviet aid, moved quickly to unify political authority in Madrid and to whip a republican army into shape, if necessary by crushing resistance from unsympathetic juntas and their militias, particularly the hated anarchists and Trotskyites. The Soviets pressured the republican legislature to make Largo Caballero prime minister, not because Largo was a Communist (he was not), but because he was the most vocal and the most charismatic Marxist leader in Spain. The Soviets thought that he would be steadfastly pro-Soviet and had openly courted him, calling him the Spanish Lenin. It was at this juncture that many foreign observers began to label the republic communist, but the republic in war was very different from what it had been in peace. The Communist party had won no seats in the 484-member legislature in 1931, 1 in 1933, and 17 in 1936. Communism had been a weak political force in prewar Spain, and came to dominate the republic only after the war began, when the USSR coupled political influence to military assistance. Moreover, Largo Caballero soon proved to be a Spaniard first and a Marxist ideologue second; he resisted further Soviet infiltration of Spanish politics. He wanted Soviet aid *for* Spain, not the sovietization *of* Spain. Although a dedicated Marxist, Largo Caballero was unwilling to be a part of the Comintern's political strategy for Europe. He was replaced by a collaborator more willing to play the puppet, Juan Negrín, but the Soviets soon lost interest in Spain. They began a steady withdrawal when their involvement, which had never been wholehearted, failed to produce the desired goal. Hugh Thomas commented:

> With crablike caution . . . Stalin seems to have reached one conclusion, and one conclusion only, about Spain; he would not permit the Republic to lose even though he would not help it to win. The mere continuance of the war would keep him free to act in any way. It might even make possible a world war in which France, Britain, Germany, and Italy would destroy themselves with Russia, the arbiter, staying outside.[7]

When it became obvious to the Soviet leaders that this war was not going to take place in the way they had hoped, aid to Spain was drastically reduced. After the agreement in Munich in September 1938, international events drew Soviet attention away from Spain and toward a reappraisal of its relationship with Nazi Germany. Spain was no longer useful, and the republic was abandoned. From that moment on, a Nationalist victory became inevitable.

The Rebel Camp

The rebels were also politically divided, but they were united in their conviction that the republic had to be destroyed. The shape that Spain would take after the overthrow would be decided later; the immediate goal was to win the war— a war the conspirators had not planned on. They had rebelled in the tradition of the pronunciamiento, characteristically a short-lived blow to the state that brought in a new regime with little bloodshed, a kind of game among soldiers who knew when to surrender. The republicans did not play the soldiers' game, however, and their resistance turned the military uprising into a full-fledged civil war. Supporting the insurgents were the classic forces of the Spanish Right: the majority of the military leadership; the monarchists (both Alfonsine and Carlist); the hierarchy of the Catholic church; the great landowners; the powerful business interests; the aristocracy; the Falange; and all of those who, without specific group identification, championed a united Spain in the tradition that dated back to the Catholic Kings.

The issue of the center against the regions caused the paradoxical realignment of some of the Catholic forces at the outbreak of the Civil War. The Catalans had been granted home rule in the form of the Generalitat in 1931, during the Red Biennium of the Second Republic. A similar request for local self-government by the Basques had been rejected. The Basque region is the most devoutly Catholic area in Spain, and during the first biennium leftist leaders feared the creation of what Indalecio Prieto called a "Vatican Gibraltar" in Spain— a deeply Catholic autonomous enclave whose first loyalty would be to the church and not to the republic. It was not until after the Civil War had broken out that Basque home rule was finally granted on October 13, 1936. In exchange for this reward from the republic, the provinces of Álava, Guipúzcoa, and Vizcaya fought on the side of the Loyalists, even though the republic remained profoundly anti-Catholic. The fourth Basque province, Navarre, fought alongside the Nationalists, who championed Catholicism but condemned regionalism. Navarre became the home base of the Carlists, and the paladins of autonomy and of the ancient fueros leagued themselves, ironically, with the rebels, who would eventually remake Spain into a rigid, unitary state.

Commitment to Catholic values was perhaps the only element that all the insurgents had in common. The dedication was little more than an unstructured spirit, however; only one of the groups taking part in the uprising had a formal ideology. The Falange Española de las Juntas de Ofensiva Nacional-Sindicalista (FE de las JONS, Spanish Phalanx of the Juntas of the National-Syndicalist Offensive) was a party pieced together by José Antonio Primo de Rivera (the son of General Primo) from two already existing fascist groups— José Antonio's own Falange Española and the Juntas de Ofensiva Nacional-Sindicalista, itself a merger of two earlier groups. It is almost impossible to make this hybrid rational. Hugh Thomas, a reknowned scholar of the Spanish Civil War, has written of José Antonio: "His speeches and writings leave the impression of a talented undergraduate who has read but not quite digested an overlong course of political theory."[8] José Antonio and his political movement were romantic (meaning fanciful, impractical, unrealistic, adventuresome, idealistic, passionate, ardent, chivalrous) and poetic. José Antonio dreamed of a unified, Catholic Spain, condemned class warfare and proselytized an authentic national syndicalism, anathematized liberalism, socialism, capitalism, and traditional conservatism, yet called for revolutionary economic reform in language usually associated with the Left and not with the Right, all the while extolling violence, bloodshed, and death.

Even though José Antonio was a handsome, charismatic, swashbuckling señorito—the kind of indulged young gentleman often admired by the Spanish gentry—his ideas held little appeal for the elite until the months immediately preceding the outbreak of the Civil War. His party did not win even a single seat in the national elections of 1936. The FE de las JONS had not hidden its distrust of the military (José Antonio had not forgotten the army's abandonment of his father in 1929), alienating this powerful body on the Right. The party's antimonarchical sentiments (an aspect of its anticonservative bias) had estranged both the Alfonsine and Carlist supporters, and its call for profound socioeconomic reform had struck fear into all of the propertied classes. Yet after the elections in February 1936, the FE de las JONS became the most militant and virulent antigovernmental force in Spain, and its ranks swelled with those horrified by the Left.

It would be interesting (but futile) to speculate about how Spain would have emerged from the Civil War if José Antonio had not been jailed by the republic in March 1936, four months before the uprising, and secretly executed on November 20, 1936. What kind of struggle for dominance would have taken place between Franco, who emerged as the absolute military and political chief of the rebels soon after the war broke out, and the man who could have become the spiritual voice of the new Spain? As we shall see in the next chapter, Franco ingeniously took the FE de las JONS, leaderless without José Antonio, and wed its amorphous and pliable beliefs to the passionate but narrow traditionalism nurtured by the Comunión Tradicionalista (Traditionalist Communion) of the Carlists to create the even more formless and pliant (and internally contradictory) Falange Española Tradicionalista y de las Juntas de Ofensiva Nacional-Sindicalista, FET y de las JONS.

The Two Ideologies

It is impossible to know with certainty why the Loyalists lost and the Nationalists won. We may conjecture, however.

Many of the ideologies that swirled within Loyalist Spain were either alien to Spanish tradition or divisive to the state and society. The Soviet communism introduced while the republic was at war was an international movement indistinguishable from the Soviet Union. Anarchism, though not indigenous, had taken deep root in Spain but was itself a fissiparous force that worked counterproductively to a consolidated republican war effort. Regionalism also acted at cross-purposes to the center, and the newly autonomous regions of Catalonia and the three Basque provinces were unable to maintain a tranquil relationship with Madrid. Most of the elements within the republic at war acted centrifugally, pulling the state apart. By contrast, the Nationalists plumbed wellsprings that were indigenously Spanish: unity, order, hierarchy, nationalism, Catholicism. The insurgents used the historical Spanish contempt—even hatred—for all things foreign as an instrument of unity. Foreign intervention did not seem to compromise these sentiments. There was no Nazi or Fascist counterpart to the Comintern, and the rebel leaders allowed no direct political control to accompany Italian or German aid. The rebels made the strong case that Nationalist Spain never sold the Spanish soul. Franco remained forever noncommittal toward his benefactors and never appeared to show them any gratitude. Thus the forces fighting for the Nationalists represented indigenous, centripetal elements in Spanish society. The strongest centrifugal element—the intensely regionalist Carlists from Navarre—had chosen between their religion and their autonomy and were committed, albeit reluctantly, to national unity.

NOTES

1. Harry Eckstein, *Division and Cohesion in Democracy* (Princeton, N.J.: Princeton University Press, 1966), p. 265.

2. Stanley Payne, *The Spanish Revolution* (New York: W. W. Norton, 1970), p. 155.

3. Salvador de Madariaga, *Spain: A Modern History* (New York: Praeger, 1958), p. 435.

4. Ibid., p. 455.

5. Ibid., pp. 524–525.

6. Raymond Carr, *Spain, 1808–1975,* 2d ed. (Oxford: Clarendon Press, 1982), p. 661.

7. Hugh Thomas, *The Spanish Civil War* (New York: Harper & Row, 1963), p. 216.

8. Ibid., p. 70.

5

The Franco Regime

The political evolution of the Franco regime can be roughly divided into four phases, each identified by basic systemic change. The first phase, 1936–1941, is almost coterminous with the Civil War; the second extends from 1942 to 1952; the third from 1953 to 1958; the fourth from 1959 to the death of Franco on November 20, 1975.[1]

THE FIRST PHASE: 1936–1941

The image that the Franco regime projected from 1936 to 1975 was established during the first three years, and very little that occurred later would alter it. Those who called the regime totalitarian based on what was said and done in Spain from 1936 to 1939 were clearly justified.

The insurgents had planned a coup d'état that would be successful within a few days, following the classic pattern of Spanish pronunciamientos. When the republic withstood the first attacks and girded itself for prolonged resistance, the rebellion turned into civil war. Franco became the supreme military commander, the generalissimo, by October 1, 1936, after a series of fortuitous events—death in battle, capture and execution, and an airplane accident—had eliminated all except one of the major Nationalist commanding officers in the early days of the uprising. The remaining general, Emilio Mola, who might have challenged Franco's newly acquired power, was forced by battlefield defeats to acquiesce to Franco, whose troops had been victorious in their first encounters with the Loyalists. Franco's unassailable military preeminence made him the inevitable choice of his fellow conspirators, who gave him supreme political power when it became apparent that the territories captured from the republicans would have to be governed until the war was over. Franco was officially made "head of government of the Spanish State" on October 1, 1936. The insurgents had already outlawed political parties on September 13, 1936, and in their place Franco created the FET y de las JONS to be Nationalist Spain's only legal political organ. He became its leader. By April 1937, Franco was commander in chief of the armed forces, head of state, head of government, and head of the single party. He became chief and sole legislator on January 30, 1938, when he was given the exclusive power to make law. His power spread as republican territory fell to the rebels, until the Nationalist victory in 1939 consolidated it throughout the country. Until his death in 1975, Franco kept all power intact, "responsible only to God and History."

Franco invalidated all laws of the republic that ran counter to his political, moral, and ethical beliefs. On March 9, 1938, strikes were forbidden by action of the Labor Charter, which was converted retroactively into the first Fundamental Law on July 26, 1947. Late in March 1938, civil marriage was banned; all marriages would henceforth be performed in the Roman Catholic church under its requirements, provisions, and prohibitions. Divorce was made illegal retroactively to 1932. Religious education became compulsory in all schools. In April 1938, the National Service of Economics and Social Reform was established to return to its original owners most of the land that had been nationalized by the republic's agrarian reform. On April 12, 1938, Franco decreed that every publication in Spain be submitted to prior censorship, a draconian measure that remained unchanged until 1966. Only certain publications of the Catholic church were exempted. On July 20, 1938, Franco ordered that with the exception of Catholic and state ceremonies, no public meeting could take place without official permission. Perhaps the most overtly totalitarian law of the new state was promulgated on February 9, 1939. The retroactive Law of Political Responsibilities made criminally liable all those who had contributed to the "red subversion" since 1934 (the year of the uprising in Asturias) and all who had actively opposed the Nationalist movement. On March 1, 1940 (eleven months after the Civil War had ended) Franco outlawed all Masonic, Communist, and anarchist organizations, and on January 25, 1941, extended the prohibition to all groups and associations not approved by the government. Again, only organizations of the Catholic church were exempted.

It was during this period of wholesale repression that the accusations of totalitarianism were hurled at Franco, who did nothing to disabuse his critics of their charges. "Our state will be the totalitarian instrument in the service of national unity,"[2] Franco announced. "Spain will be organized within a fully totalitarian concept through those national institutions that assure her totality, her unity, and her continuity."[3] On the second anniversary of the rebellion, Franco proclaimed in his message to the Spanish people that "in the place of a neutered state with no ideals will be substituted a totalitarian state with the mission to give direction to the people."[4]

Domestically and internationally, Franco supported others with totalitarian leanings. His first (and perhaps only) confidant was his brother-in-law, Ramón Serrano Súñer, a militant pro-Nazi whom Franco appointed minister of the interior in charge of internal security from 1938 to 1942. Franco joined the Anti-Comintern Pact on March 21, 1939, a week before the end of the Civil War, and signed a secret treaty of friendship with Hitler. When Germany invaded Poland in September 1936, Spain declared itself neutral, but left its seaports and airports open to the Germans and Italians. As the war swept spectacularly to the advantage of the Axis powers between 1939 and 1941, Franco moved from neutrality to a more activist policy of nonbelligerency, and in June 1941, Spain sent a voluntary air unit, the División Azul (Blue Division) to fight with the Germans against the Soviet Union.

THE SECOND PHASE: 1942–1952

When it became apparent after the ill-fated Nazi invasion of the Soviet Union in June 1941 that the Axis powers, which had assisted Franco and made his victory possible, would be defeated in World War II, the caudillo began to retreat from the totalitarianism that would be unacceptable to the victorious world of the Allies. Spain after 1942 was no longer a totalitarian system. It could not be compared to the Nazi system in Germany nor even to the more benign Fascist system in Italy. Present-day students of politics may consider the distinctions once made between totalitarian systems and authoritarian systems like Franco's to be quaint, but these differences were fundamental. Authoritarian states, irrespective of how cruel they were, were considered to be far less heinous than totalitarian ones.

Franco had always maintained that the Spanish model of any system would be made from Spanish cloth cut to Spanish measure, and even when declaring his totalitarian convictions during the Civil War, he also said that Spain was unlike any other system because of its Catholicism. This was a valid point, as no thoroughly totalitarian system would have tolerated a force that it could not control. The Catholic doctrine that Franco claimed his regime was based on was determined not by Franco in Madrid but by the Pope in Rome. Moreover, according to Franco's belief, the salvation of the soul in the keeping of the church was the primary purpose of human existence, not service to the state—the basic tenet of totalitarianism. Nor did Franco govern through charisma and terror as did most totalitarian leaders. Franco's power remained absolute until the moment of his death, but he used his power to balance or mix those groups and institutions without whose support he would have been unable to rule: the army, the hierarchy of the Catholic church in Spain, the FET y de las JONS (later the National Movement), the monarchists (Alfonsine, Carlist, and later Juan Carlist), the economic oligarchy, the aristocracy, and the Opus Dei (a semisecret Catholic lay organization).[5] These groups set the limits of the Spanish political game. Within these limits Franco skillfully used his power to keep any group from permanent ascendancy, maintaining his own superior power as indispensable to the stability of the system. Franco juggled a kind of political pluralism that belonged neither in a democracy nor in a totalitarian regime.

During the second phase Franco shifted away from his pro-Axis policy. Serrano Súñer was convinced to go into permanent political retirement (where he stayed for the rest of his life), and in June 1942, Franco appointed the pro-British Count of Jordana to be foreign minister. In October 1943, the generalissimo also moved from nonbelligerency back to neutrality, and withdrew the Blue Division from Germany. It must be conceded, however, that throughout his courtship of the Germans, Franco made no concessions to Hitler's entreaties, particularly concerning Operation Felix, the plan to seal the western Mediterranean by capturing Gibraltar and controlling North Africa. This operation, which could have changed the outcome of World War II, would have necessitated a march across Spain, a plan that Franco refused to even consider. When Hitler and Franco met at Hendaye on the Spanish-French border on October 23, 1940, the stubbornness of the always proper and unflappable generalissimo was such that Hitler later remarked that he would prefer to have several teeth pulled than to go through another session with Franco.

On the domestic front, Franco formulated the Fundamental Laws that would make up his "constitution." The Labor Charter, the first Fundamental Law, had been created in 1938, in part to forbid strikes and to outlaw unions. It also guaranteeed job security, regulated salaries, and controlled the relationship between employer and employee. Labor and management were compelled to join the official state syndicates, designed to coordinate all economic activity, and end the conflictual relationship that Franco claimed had corrupted the economic process in capitalist societies.[6] In theory, the Labor Charter treated employers and employees evenhandedly; in practice it greatly favored employers. As an example, most professional and commercial organizations were allowed to operate, although labor unions had been banned.

The second Fundamental Law (July 17, 1942) set up the Cortes or legislature, but representation in this body was severely limited. The *procuradores* (an antique, predemocratic term for legislators) were indirectly elected from municipal councils, syndicates, and official state organizations (such as professional associations and universities), the great majority of whose members were appointed by Franco. Moreover, the generalissimo remained chief (if no longer sole) legislator, with the power to annul any law that the Cortes might have the temerity to pass against his will (this never occurred, however). On July 17, 1945, Franco proclaimed the third Fundamental Law, the Charter of the Spanish People, the Spanish equivalent of a bill of rights. Before this decree there had been no constitutional guarantees to protect citizens from the dictates of the FET y de las JONS that policed all civil rights. The guarantees in the charter were still limited, as these rights could be suspended if their enjoyment threatened or undermined the "national, spiritual, or social unity of Spain," all of which was interpreted by Franco alone.

In order to give the people some role in the political process, Franco proclaimed the fourth Fundamental Law on October 22, 1945. The Referendum Law allowed the Spaniards to approve or disapprove political matters of transcendental importance. A referendum could only be presented by Franco, however, and there was no guarantee that the verdict of the people would be carried out if it were contrary to Franco's purpose. The fifth Fundamental Law was promulgated on July 6, 1947. The Law of Succession in the Headship of State declared Spain to be a monarchy, with the monarch to be designated by Franco alone at a date of his choosing. The law was approved in referendum by 73 per cent of the electorate.

Despite the transparency of the Fundamental Laws, the referendum approving the Law of Succession was the first manifestation of popular support for the regime and the first step toward establishing an identifiable and measurable rational-legal legitimacy. The referendum not only approved the restoration of the monarchy and the succession to Franco but also retroactively ratified all the previous Fundamental Laws. If the Fundamental Laws were designed in part to win approval for the Franco regime from the democracies, however, they were created in vain. Spain remained a pariah nation, denied a seat in the United Nations and in all of its subsidiary organizations and, with the exception of Argentina, deprived of diplomatic relations with the major nations of the world, which refused to exchange ambassadors. Spain was alone and destitute. Shattered by the Civil War, in 1947 the Spanish economy was still in ruins.

THE THIRD PHASE: 1953–1958

Franco's wife always said that God's hand had guided the fortuitous events that resulted in Franco's ascent from among his fellow conspirators to become the supreme ruler of Spain. It was the United States, however, that intervened in the early 1950s, after the Cold War—and the Korean War in particular—had seemingly vindicated Franco's ceaseless warnings that communism was mankind's most dangerous enemy.

By the late 1940s the Spanish economy was near collapse.[7] Spain's isolation from the family of nations had forced it into autarky, or economic self-sufficiency. For a nation rich in resources, this policy might have worked longer, but Spain was poor in resources, devastated by war, and unable to attract the foreign investment it needed to rebuild its economy. Autarky soon ran its course, and the nation was in extremis. Before the situation had deteriorated into nationwide penury and hunger, however, the United States unwittingly came to the rescue.

In the early 1950s, the U.S. military was seeking bases from which to encircle the USSR and secure U.S. defense. Spain, with its control of the Strait of Gibraltar, was indispensable, and the United States came shopping with enormous resources in hand. Franco welcomed the offer, and made extraordinary demands for money and arms in exchange for air bases at Morón, Torrejón, and Zaragoza, and a naval base at Rota. Whatever the price, the Americans needed Franco more than he needed them (or at least that is the convincing pose that the generalissimo maintained), and they paid dearly, $225 million ($141 million for military and $84 million for nonmilitary purposes) for starters.[8] The agreement with the United States was signed on September 26, 1953, just a month after Franco had signed a new concordat with the Vatican to replace the one signed in 1851. Through these negotiations, Franco's Spain was recognized as an equal by the world's most powerful democratic nation and by the world's most powerful spiritual institution. The symbolism of this dual endorsement was not lost on the world. On December 15, 1955, Spain was admitted to the United Nations. Its ostracism had come to an end.

Franco accepted the largesse without gratitude. He did not alter the regime to make it more appealing to either his material or his spiritual benefactor, but profound systemic change was about to take place whether he wanted it or not. Franco could not have foreseen the transformations that would take place in Catholicism as a result of the Second Vatican Council opened by Pope John XXIII on December 7, 1965. Doctrinal liberalization out of Rome would undermine the philosophical structure of the Spanish regime. Concerning his material benefactor, however, Franco should have realized that the impact of the United States with its aggressive society and economy could not have been withstood by even a strong and self-confident nation, much less by a destitute and crippled Spain, still suffering from the wounds of the Civil War and innocent to the ways of the modern world. Franco's provincialism and his refusal to learn from what he considered alien sources (i.e., any source outside of Spain and any source inside of Spain of which he disapproved) made it impossible for him to understand that the magnitude of U.S. assistance and the U.S. presence in Spain would have inevitable repercussions. American money, tourists, and military and civilian personnel poured into Spain, followed by money and tourists from around the world. The shock of modernity set changes in motion that totally altered Spanish life.

THE FOURTH PHASE: 1959–1975

Franco's anticommunist propaganda, which ended only with his death, had been matched at the beginning of his regime by anticapitalist propaganda. "Bourgeois capitalists spill blood while making fabulous profit from Spanish lives."[9]

Franco had proclaimed that the Nationalist victory in the Civil War would lead to "the triumph of economic principles in conflict with old liberal theories by whose myths colonialism had been established in many sovereign states."[10] His anti-capitalist animus had been enthusiastically shared by the men who had helped him organize the FET y de las JONS in 1936. After 1953, when Spain finally had the funds to begin restructuring the economy, the old guard of the Falange prepared to put its ideology into practice. Yet Franco decreed otherwise, and in an about-face that surprised the world and stunned his fellow Falangists into silence, he embraced capitalism. The Spanish economy would be rebuilt upon a capitalist foundation, not upon the corporativist base borrowed from Mussolini's Italy that Franco had originally planned to emulate. With no explanation Franco changed his mind, if not his heart, but the leaders of the FET y de las JONS remained faithful to the beliefs they had embraced in the 1930s, even though in Italy these beliefs had been buried along with the fascist regime as a result of World War II. In order to ease the blow to the party's economic principles, Franco underscored the party's political preeminence in the sixth Fundamental Law, the Principles of the National Movement (the new name for the FET y de las JONS), which he declared permanent and unalterable on May 17, 1958.

Franco placed the economic direction of Spain in the hands of a group of technocrats who belonged, most of them, to Opus Dei (Latin for God's Work), a semisecret Catholic lay organization that recruited primarily from Spain's upper middle and upper classes.[11] Many of these men had been educated in graduate schools specializing in finance, business administration, and economics in the United States, France, and Great Britain, and they shared philosophical convictions that reconciled modern capitalism with Catholicism. Placing their expertise at the service of the Spanish state, these technocrats performed the miracle that brought Spain economically into the postwar world. Their accomplishments are discussed in Chapter 12.

While the economic and social changes of the 1960s were taking place, Franco moved to undergird his regime politically and at the same time to loosen the restraints under which the Spanish people had long chafed. By this time, they were beginning to express their discontent. On December 14, 1966, Franco presented the seventh and final Fundamental Law for approval through referendum. Of the 21,803,397 eligible voters, 19,466,709 voted "yes." In effect, the Organic Law of the State closed the door on the past and actualized the completed political system whose structure Franco had begun to build in the midst of the Civil War. The law reconciled the inconsistencies that existed among the earlier Fundamental Laws, reworded the few vestiges of terminology that could be called totalitarian, and continued liberalization (or the retreat from authoritarianism, if the reader prefers). It provided for the direct election of representatives to the Cortes (by the heads of families—male or female, not through universal suffrage), and separated the role of head of state from that of head of government (although Franco continued to act as both until 1973). As of January 10, 1967, the day the Organic Law went into operation, the political system was ready for posterity in the form Franco considered to be essentially and permanently fixed. On July 22, 1969, Franco announced that his successor would be Juan Carlos, bypassing the prince's father, Don Juan de Borbón. The choice further consolidated the power of the Opus Dei technocrats who had supported the prince against his father. Don Juan was the choice of the leadership of the National Movement, whose authority Franco had once again diminished.

Retreat from Authoritarianism

Even before the Organic Law was approved Franco had begun to ease the reins held tight on the people since the early years of the Civil War. The press law of April 29, 1938, was at last replaced by the new Press and Publishing Law of March 18, 1966, which abolished prior censorship. On June 28, 1967, the Cortes approved the Law on Religious Freedom, which declared that Spaniards with non-Catholic religious beliefs could no longer incur prejudice before the law. Under its terms, civil marriage would be allowed for non-Catholics, participation in religious ceremonies in the army and in the schools would no longer be obligatory, and non-Catholic religious associations could organize and publicly practice their faith.

The liberalization did not undercut opposition to the regime. On the contrary, opposition grew in proportion to the success of the economic miracle. The earliest opposition to the Franco regime had virtually been eradicated in the years immediately following the end of the Civil War, when the defeated Loyalists, especially the Communists, sought to destroy the regime through guerrilla warfare. The enemies of the new state were ruthlessly hunted down and exterminated, and an airless peace was finally achieved in Spain. After the hermetic seal was broken in the 1950s, Spaniards became haltingly but increasingly restless. Economic well-being, which spread to a larger and larger number of people during the next two decades, did not stifle demands for freedom. Franco had thought that the newly affluent middle class and the increasingly prosperous working class could be bought off by the liberalization represented in the new laws. The new middle class would not be assuaged, however, and the working class was dissatisfied with its economic progress. Although their standard of living had undeniably improved since autarky, Spanish workers had not yet caught up with laborers in the rest of Western Europe, and many aspired to rise to the middle class.

There had always been opposition to the Franco regime, even after the guerrillas were destroyed and the system became entrenched in the mid-1940s. There was what Juan Linz called the semiopposition, "those groups that are not dominant or represented in the governing group but are willing to participate in power without fundamentally challenging the regime."[12] For example, the Falange became part of the semiopposition when Franco rejected its approach to economic rejuvenation and embraced the theories of the Opus Dei instead. Any of the major supporting groups of the regime (army, church, Falange) temporarily out of Franco's favor became part of the semiopposition. Beyond the semiopposition was the alegal opposition, made up of those working to

change the system peacefully. They were too estranged from
the regime to be brought into the ruling elite (though they
often maintained personal friendships with its members), nor
would they have accepted the invitation had they been asked
to join. Yet these dissidents were able to pursue their careers
only because of the regime's forbearance; they were vulnerable
not only to the whims of Franco but also to accusations that
they were opportunists who wanted the best of two mutually
exclusive worlds. University professors like Enrique Tierno
Galván, Antonio Tóvar, and José Luis Aranguren and jour-
nalists like Joaquín Ruiz Giménez are examples of the alegal
opposition. Giménez had been minister of education from
1951 to 1956, but broke with the regime after 1956. He joined
the alegal opposition and later founded *Cuadernos para el
diálogo* (Workbooks for dialogue), probably the most influential
popular magazine in Spain critical of the regime. Beyond the
alegal opposition was the illegal opposition of underground
political parties and the secret Workers' Commissions.

Opposition to the regime in the 1950s and 1960s oscillated
between the alegal and the illegal. It came primarily from
three sources: university students, labor, and the church.
Students in the late 1950s and early 1960s had begun to reel
under the heady impact of foreign ideas and foreign peoples
pouring into Spain after Franco opened the country to the
world in 1953. In their quest for independence and intellectual
freedom, these young men and women increasingly resisted
compulsory membership in the government-sponsored university syndicates, apologists for the regime. Franco was
compelled to treat the students gingerly—an approach he did
not find congenial—and he grudgingly granted them limited
freedom to create their own university organizations. His
dilemma was that the vast majority of Spanish university
students at that time came from the upper middle and upper
classes. Clamping down too harshly on student restiveness
might harm the children of Franco's own supporters.

Franco's approach to labor demands was less tolerant.
The working classes and their representatives—the Communist, Socialist, and Anarchist parties, and the trade unions—
had been Franco's most dogged enemies during the Civil War.

His first Fundamental Law, the Labor Charter, had been created in large measure to break labor's back by forbidding strikes, outlawing all free trade unions, and forcing the workers into the official state syndicates. In time, however, particularly after the mid-1950s, labor began to organize clandestinely; Communists and radical Catholics created the secret Workers' Commissions that eventually infiltrated the Jurados de Empresa, the quasirepresentative bodies created in 1953 within the syndicates to give labor a somewhat stronger voice.[13] The regime even tolerated certain nonpolitical strikes. Franco remained adamant, however, refusing the workers' fundamental demand: the right to organize free trade unions openly. At the time of his death, Franco was no closer to accepting this demand than he had been in 1938, when he took his first stand against the working class.

The Dilemma of Vatican II

The liberalization within the Catholic church in Spain presented Franco with his most painful dilemma. His regime had been based upon classic, conservative Catholic doctrines and had been supported by the church hierarchy in Spain, who had remained silent in the face of political and economic repression. In fact, Franco had claimed that because of the church his regime had never been totalitarian. In exchange for its support, the church was allowed to shape and control the ethics, morality, and education of the country. So long as the Vatican did not fundamentally restructure its own thinking on politics and economics, the Spanish regime was philosophically secure. If the church were to change, however, then the Spanish system would also have to change to remain loyal to the teachings of the church.

The Second Vatican Council forced the universal church to recognize the reality of urban, secular, industrial life. The individual's political and economic rights, claims for a share of the good things of this world, and demands for political and economic freedom became the rallying cry of the progressives, whose voices shook the Vatican assembly and shaped its decrees. The cry was taken up by the younger, liberal clergy within the Spanish church, and the fundamental elements of Francoism came under public scrutiny and attack. How could Franco silence their voices without challenging the institution whose teachings were the basis of his regime? Franco could not keep out the new doctrines and directives and still proclaim himself a son of "Holy Mother Church." This was a dilemma Franco never reconciled.

By the early 1960s, a fourth source of opposition—the regionalists—had grown increasingly insistent. Against this opposition, Franco unleashed repression so severe that many Spaniards feared the regime was returning to the mood and the tactics of the early 1940s. The voice of the regionalists— the Basques, Catalans, and Galicians—had been raised in vain at Franco. Angered by his refusal to entertain their pleas for permission to speak their own language and to honor their own culture and heritage, they turned to violent action.

In what could be labeled his most shortsighted policy, in the name of national unity, Franco forbade any native language other than Spanish to be written or spoken anywhere in Spain, even in the privacy of one's home. National unity was perhaps Franco's most relentless obsession, and although one may sympathize with his desire to hold Spaniards together, his actions were intolerable. A suppressed people will eventually explode. History teaches us that lesson, but Franco refused to acknowledge history (though he once declared himself "responsible only to God and History"). The historic fueros in whose name the regionalists made their demands were rejected by Franco as an anachronism in modern Spain.

The most notorious and brutal of the regionalist groups was the Euzkadi Ta Azkatasuna (ETA, Basque Fatherland and Liberty). This and other clandestine organizations are discussed in Chapter 10. The ETA had been created in 1952 as a propaganda organ of the outlawed Basque Nationalist Party, the PNV. In 1958, the ETA broke away from the PNV and became avowedly Marxist and revolutionary. Because its members spoke for the freedom desired by most of their fellow Basques, they were tolerated and often admired despite their reign of terror and assassination that still goes on today. The most daring operation carried out while Franco was alive was the assassination of Admiral Luis Carrero Blanco on December 20, 1973, only six months following his appointment as Franco's first prime minister.

Already in the 1960s there had been spectacular trials of ETA members and other groups accused of killing police officers, soldiers, and civil guards. The trials were held before military tribunals, and for all practical purposes the verdicts were determined even before the opening statements of the defense were made. The world responded in shock at the blatant disregard of justice, but world opinion notwithstanding, three men were executed in 1963. The next trials, probably the ones that received the most publicity, took place in Burgos in 1970. Franco commuted the sentences of the convicted terrorists, probably in response to world opinion, yet in March 1974 he allowed a young convicted member of another terrorist group, the Iberian Liberation Movement, to be executed by garrote, an ancient instrument of execution by strangulation, formerly used for those guilty of certain kinds of violent crimes.

In August 1975, a new antiterrorist law made the death penalty obligatory for those convicted of terrorist acts that caused the death of a member of the police, the security or the armed forces, or that resulted in the death or mutilation of a kidnap victim. The law also stipulated that all political groups of communist, anarchist, or separatist tendencies and any other group that recommended or used violence as an instrument of social and political action would be subject to maximum penalties. Moreover, it was made a crime to condone or defend acts of terrorism, to criticize a sentence passed on a convicted terrorist, or to call for solidarity with a convicted terrorist. Punishment could include imprisonment for up to two years, a fine of 50,000 to 500,000 pesetas, or both.

That same month four trials of terrorists resulted in the conviction of eleven men and women. Five were executed (all men) and six were reprieved by Franco's order. Three months later, in November 1975, the generalissimo was dead. He left his fellow Spaniards apprehensive and fearful, with memories of the Civil War recalled by the caudillo's last official commands, an ironic epitaph for the man who in 1964 celebrated the quarter-century anniversary of the end of the war under a banner extolling "25 Years of Peace."

NOTES

1. See E. Ramón Arango, *The Spanish Political System: Franco's Legacy* (Boulder, Colo.: Westview Press, 1978).

2. Jorge Solé-Tura, *Introducción al régimen político Español* (Barcelona: Ediciones Ariel, Espulgues de Llobregat, 1971), pp. 23–24.

3. *Palabras de Franco* (Bilbao: Editora Nacional, 1937), p. 15.

4. *Palabras del Caudillo* (Madrid: Ediciones de la Vicesecretariá de Educación Popular, 1953), p. 315.

5. The proper name of the Opus Dei is Societas Sacerdotalis Sanctae Crucis (Priestly Society of the Holy Cross). It is a secular institute of the Catholic church, headquartered in Rome, with a worldwide membership. It was founded by a Spaniard, José Mariá Escrivá de Balaguer y Albás, in order to pursue "God's work" not by withdrawing from the world into convents and monasteries, but by remaining in the world pursuing a secular occupation while personally leading a dedicated Christian life and influencing others by work and deed. It is not a religious order; there are no canonically binding vows. However, most of its highest ranking members—unmarried, university educated, with no physical handicaps, coming from good social background—do take noncanonical vows of poverty, chastity, and obedience and most often live together in special but anonymous residences. Its detractors called the society the "white Freemasonry" and the "Holy Mafia."

6. The syndicates were created to be one of the three basic groups of society in which Spaniards would share common experiences and values. The other two were the family and the local community. These three associations reflected Franco's organic concept of society as made up of interlocking, mutually supportive, noncompetitive parts. The syndicates were designed to provide employers and employees with a forum in which to meet and solve problems not as opponents or antagonists but as the obverse and reverse face of a single organization, whose unity of purpose should totally outweigh whatever differences might exist within it. All employers and employees in a particular economic activity were members of a single syndicate organized in two sections, one for employers and one for employees. There were twenty-nine

syndicates, representing all economic activities except the professions, which had their own organizations, civil servants, and domestics. The syndicates were organized at the community, provincial, and national levels in a kind of democratic centralism, with the higher level indirectly chosen from the lower. The national syndicates were not autonomous entitites, however; they were completely under the control of the state. Moreover, in the operation of the syndicates at all levels, the great advantage lay with the employers and not with the employees, whom Franco deeply mistrusted as a group.

7. See Chapter 12 for a sustained evaluation of the Spanish economy.

8. In the first ten years, the United States poured into Spain more than $1.5 billion in economic assistance and more than $500 million in military aid. The pact was renewed in 1963 and 1970, and in 1976 its status was raised from executive agreement to treaty. On January 24, 1976, the United States and Spain signed a Treaty of Friendship and Cooperation.

9. *Palabras del Caudillo*, pp. 26–27.

10. Ibid., p. 118.

11. See note 6 above.

12. Juan Linz, "Opposition to and Under an Authoritarian Regime: The Case of Spain," in Robert A. Dahl, ed., *Regimes and Opposition* (New Haven, Conn.: Yale University Press, 1973), p. 191.

13. The Jurados de Empresa were created in 1953 and established in every firm employing more than fifty workers. They operated within a single firm (in contrast to the syndicates, which represented all firms of a similar nature in a particular geographic area). Initially, the Jurados' role was primarily to communicate workers' viewpoints and complaints to management. Their role expanded after 1957, when the Franco regime allowed limited collective bargaining to take place at the level of the individual firm.

Part 2

Return to Democracy

6

The Transition

The events of the "transition"—the Spanish term for the period that began at Franco's death in November 1975—can best be understood against the background of the preceding two years between the assassination of Carrero Blanco in December 1973 and the demise of the caudillo. Prime Minister Carrero's administration, which began in June 1973, was a reactionary response from a system that felt control slipping out of its hands. The regime was assailed from all sides: by students; by labor; by the more liberal church; by regional extremists; by certain elements of the press; and by the very class that had most profited from Franco's socioeconomic policies after the early 1950s—the new urban middle class. Franco's liberalization program had not stopped dissent. The workings of the more permissive press law of 1966, the election of family representatives to the Cortes after 1967, the possibility of some degree of political expression within the National Movement after 1967, and the tacit toleration of certain nonpolitical strikes relaxed the suffocating grip of the regime yet also emboldened dissidents to demand more freedom. Unless the regime were prepared to use total repression and return the state to the climate of the years following the end of the Civil War, more change was inevitable. Franco's appointment of Carrero appeared to many to indicate a regression, for Carrero went into office calling for "unity of power and coordination of functions." Raymond Carr wrote: "It was under the bleak authoritarian rule of Carrero that the peace of Franco came to an end."[1]

93

Carrero's assassination by Basque terrorists less than six months after his appointment may have persuaded Franco to think again. The generalissimo replaced Carrero with Carlos Arias Navarro, the tough, politically orthodox mayor of Madrid, yet Arias's first address to the Cortes as prime minister on February 12, 1974, gave hope that renewed liberalization might occur and the right to form political associations be granted. This was the key demand of the opposition, whether the alegal opposition in Spain, the illegal opposition in Spain, or the opposition of Spanish political organizations in exile. In his speech, Arias promised a new statute of associations, and as nothing took place at this level of Spanish politics without Franco's approval, obviously this opening was the caudillo's own cautious venture. Reaction to the proposal was swift. On the right, it was condemned by diehard Francoists, more conservative even than Franco, for whom all change was tantamount to chaos. On the left it was criticized by those for whom only a total break with the past would suffice. Conservatives who wanted things to stay more or less the same after Franco died but who wanted Spain to look better internationally supported this basically cosmetic proposal.

Franco's illness at midyear altered the pace of the anticipated liberalization, but other internal crises had already poisoned the atmosphere and undermined confidence in Arias's pledge. In March, the regime executed a young Catalan terrorist amidst outcries urging clemency from throughout Spain and from the rest of Europe, and in February the bishop of Bilbao was put under house arrest for speaking out in a sermon about the use of the forbidden Basque language. (Pressure from an incensed Vatican put the bishop back in his pulpit.) It was under these circumstances that Juan Carlos became acting head of state on July 1, 1974, with Franco too sick to govern. Perhaps the statute of associations could have become law while the prince stood in for the caudillo, but action was stopped because of the interim sovereign's lack of experience; the fierce opposition of the Francoist diehards (later christened the "bunker" by the media), who resisted even the liberalization that originated with Franco; and the natural conservatism of Arias, for whom change had never been congenial and who was reluctant to move while his mentor was incapacitated. It was not until three months after Franco resumed office on September 2, 1974, that the associations bill was finally passed by the Cortes, but the law was a sham. It provided for political participation only through associations whose legality would be judged by the National Movement itself. There would be no alternative political opinions; the associations would instead resemble chapels within a single church.

Even before the statute became law, however, opposition to the regime had begun to swell. In July 1974 the Democratic Junta was created in Paris, made up of Communists, a branch of the Socialist party, the Carlists (who were still claiming the throne for their pretender not only against Juan Carlos but against his father, Don Juan, as well), and representatives of the outlawed Workers' Commissions. Its platform called for *ruptura* (total break, one of the great catchwords of the transition), demanding the immediate dismantling of the National Movement and the syndicates, the legalization of all political parties and trade unions, and the election of a constituent assembly whose first task would be to decide whether the new regime would be a constitutional monarchy or a republic. In Spain, terrorist activity exploded with such virulence that in April 1975 the Basque region was placed under martial law, an action that enflamed even those Basques (the great majority of the population) who condemned violence. In August 1975, the new antiterrorist law made the death penalty mandatory for convicted terrorists and specified that all terrorists would be tried in military courts.

By mid-1975, members of the nonviolent political opposition were organizing within Spain. The platform of Democratic Convergence linked in common cause the Socialist party (PSOE); the Social Democrats of Dionisio Ridruejo, a former Falangist who had broken with the regime in 1942; the Democratic Left, headed by Joaquín Ruiz Giménez; the Carlists (who had abandoned the Democratic Junta); the PNV (the moderate Basque nationalist party); and other small regionalist parties. The rightist Christian Democrats and the

Liberals did not affiliate with the Democratic Convergence but remained sympathetic. Within the political elite itself, several highly placed men, cabinet ministers among them, began writing a column under the pseudonym *Tácito*. Published in the newspaper *Ya*, the column supported *reforma*, another of the great catchwords. Among the Tácitos were Federico Silva Muñoz (minister of public works from 1966 to 1970), Pio Cabanillas (appointed minister of information and tourism in 1974), and José María Areilza (an early Falangist, at various times Franco's ambassador to Argentina, France, and the United States, and minister of foreign affairs from December 1975 to July 1976). It was Arielza who coined the widely repeated expression of the "civilized right" to describe his brand of conservatism. In June 1975, the Unión del Pueblo Español (Union of the Spanish People) was created, initially under the chairmanship of Adolfo Suárez, to become the voice of *continuismo* (still another catchword). This voice stressed that meaningful liberalization—a kind of democratization without democracy—could take place while maintaining the basic system intact after Franco's death.

CONSTITUTIONAL MONARCHY

On November 20, 1975, Juan Carlos, who had become head of state again on October 1 when the generalissimo's demise seemed imminent, became the king of Spain. His power was almost identical to what Franco had held. At this moment, the transition began. At first it appeared that transition would be synonymous with continuismo, for Juan Carlos maintained Arias as prime minister. For the second time, Arias promised a new statute of associations, but his address to the Cortes in January 1976 sounded more like homage to the past than hope for the future. No mention was made of regional reform, the repeal of the hated antiterrorist statute, or change in the syndicalist strucure; and even before legislative action could begin on the legalization of political parties, Arias informed the country that neither the Communist nor separatist parties would ever be tolerated. Violence engulfed Spain, particularly in the Basque provinces, and political opposition to the new regime consolidated to form the Democratic Coordination that confederated the Democratic Junta and the Platform of Democratic Convergence. This time even those Christian Democrats who had held aloof earlier joined the forces that opposed not only the government but also the members of the bunker, who pledged resistance to any change whatsoever and championed a return to the "regime of July 18" (the day the Civil War broke out in 1936). On June 9, 1976, the new Law of Political Associations was passed by the Cortes. It provided that the legality of associations (Communist and separatist excluded) would no longer be determined by the National Movement but by the Ministry of the Interior. Yet in an astonishingly illogical—even perverse—omission, the Cortes failed to amend those articles of the penal code that forbade all political activity. Continuismo seemed dead. Arias resigned on July 1, 1976, and the king appointed Adolfo Suárez to succeed him.

The precise details of what happened next will not be known until biographies, autobiographies, and memoirs appear, and even then the full story may not be revealed. Conjecture swirls about the role of Juan Carlos, who, one must remember, was legally the absolute ruler of Spain until the new democratic constitution went into effect in December 1978. Nevertheless, the king assumed the role of a constitutional monarch after he appointed Adolfo Suárez to replace Arias Navarro. At the time of Franco's death almost nothing was known about Juan Carlos' political convictions. Little in his training, carefully orchestrated by Franco, or in his very proper behavior during the years of his apprenticeship would indicate latent democratic feelings, nor did his comportment during his brief tenure as head of state in 1974 gave any inkling of this. If he had always preferred the role of constitutional monarch, why had he retained Arias Navarro, who was devoted to Franco and Francoism and who was identified with continuisimo? Would Juan Carlos have been happy with continuismo if the Cortes had depenalized political activity? At what point did Suárez enter into the monarch's ken? Why did the king turn to Suárez and not to men like Areilza or Fraga Iribarne who had been bruited as model prime ministers?

There was little in Suárez's past to explain his selection for what would be an unprecedented role in Spanish history. Suárez was not that prominent a politician. His socioeconomic background placed him far below the summits of society and power from which leaders had often had been chosen in Franco's Spain, yet he had risen to be secretary-general of the National Movement, automatically making him a cabinet minister and thus linking him to the caudillo. Moreover, he had been identified with continuismo as the former head of the Union of the Spanish People, and continuismo had been dealt a mortal blow. How did two crypto-democrats find each other? When and how did Juan Carlos and Suárez exchange views and discover their compatibility? Did they have some private agreement whose distant goal was the democratization of Spain? At this point, no one has published the information to answer these questions.

What is clear is the accomplishments of the king and his prime minister, which were nothing short of revolutionary (meaning lexically "a complete and marked change in something") and miraculous given the odds against them. Together they embraced democracy and set out on a course that rejected any attempt to revive continuismo. The reforms they adopted emerged out of the extant Fundamental Laws of the Franco regime and initially followed their provisions to the letter, yet eventually legally dismantled both the laws and the regime and created a democratic, constitutional monarchy. The idea of a republic was never entertained.

The immobilists of the old regime and the *rupturistas* attacked the program—the former because for them all change was anathema (they had equally opposed continuismo); the latter because they believed change had to emerge from the ashes of Francoism, not from its living laws and institutions. The rupturistas also demanded that the people have the option to choose between monarchism and republicanism. But the rupturistas had no alternative but to accept the Juan Carlos–Suárez formula. They had no power base for resistance, and rejecting the plan would play into the hands of the immobilists. To call for a republic, as some continued to do, particularly the Communists and the Socialists, would taunt the military beyond forbearance. The only thing that kept the armed forces contained during this hazardous period was their devotion and loyalty to Juan Carlos, who was not only the king but also Franco's heir. The *nature* of the monarchy—absolutist or constitutional—was of secondary importance to the military; the *existence* of a monarchy was beyond question. A peaceful transition from dictatorship to democracy could take place only if the throne continued to command the allegiance of the armed forces, without whose support the immobilists were powerless to prevent reform.

As they pursued their democratic goal, Juan Carlos and Suárez maneuvered to keep the opposition from both the Right and the Left either off balance or assuaged. The king replaced some military leaders known to be unsympathetic to liberalization and continued to issue amnesty decrees for political prisoners, a policy he had initiated while Arias Navarro was premier. This was particularly designed to calm the Basques who along with the Catalans were granted, again by royal decree, the right to use their own language for the first time since 1939. In the same month (December 1976), the king abolished the Court of Public Order in a decree stipulating that in the future all judicial action involving terrorism would take place in regular courts, not in military tribunals.

THE ELECTIONS OF 1977

The greatest accomplishment of the first six months of collaboration between Juan Carlos and Suárez was the Law of Political Reform, which the prime minster announced on September 10, 1976, and which the Cortes passed on November 16, 1976. In effect, the law ended the dictatorship and called for the creation of a new bicameral legislature, elected by universal suffrage, that would act as a constituent assembly. In accordance with Francoist Fundamental Law, the statute was submitted to the Spanish people in the referendum held on December 16, 1976. Of the 78 percent of the electorate who took part, 94.2 percent gave their approval.

The overwhelming vote of the people in favor of reform was not surprising. What was surprising was the overwhelming vote of the Cortes that put the democratization into motion. In the Cortes, 425 procuradores were in favor, 59 were against, and 13 abstained in a legislature that less than six months earlier had thwarted continuismo by refusing to depenalize political activity. In November, the procuradores voted the Cortes out of existence; it would continue to function only until the election of the constituent assembly took place. The politics of persuasion that brought about this phenomenal about-face remains in great part hidden. The roles of the king and the prime minister were preeminent, but their strategy has yet to be fully revealed. We do know that Suárez openly courted the opposition and created an atmosphere of trust and cooperation. Shortly after he took office, in an unprecedented fraternal gesture he met with Socialist leader Felipe González, whose party was still officially committed to republicanism. In September, Suárez conferred with the senior officers of the military and later consulted with most of the other leaders of the opposition. Once again, these forces had consolidated and expanded in October 1976 to form the Platform of Democratic Organizations, confronting the government with the most united front the opposition had yet amassed. Suárez acceded to most of the platform's demands but only agreed to implement them before the general election, not before the referendum as the dissident leaders had wanted.

During the first six months of 1977, Suárez and the king prepared the country for the first free elections since 1939, set for June 15. They began to remove the restraints of the Franco regime, fulfilling their promises to the opposition. In February 1977, the first group of political parties, including the Socialist party, was legalized. On March 16, the right to strike was established, and on March 30 the Cortes approved a law permitting the organization of free trade unions. Less than a month later, three major unions submitted their statutes and began operation. On April 1 the National Movement was abolished; on April 11 the Communist party was legalized, perhaps the most dangerous action of the entire transition. The military had been schooled to see the Communists as the greatest evil in modern society, and their annihilation had been the primary rationale for the Civil War. Legalizing the Communist party could spark the military elite to overthrow the fledgling regime; not to legalize the party would place restrictions on the democratic process even before it began, resulting in what the phrasemakers called "democracy with adjectives." This issue was preeminent even for those democratic reformers who abhorred Marxism, and it became symbolic of the open society emerging in Spain that, it was hoped, would be strong enough to accommodate and survive any ideology. The military did not revolt primarily because Juan Carlos held it firmly in his grip, compelling the armed forces by the sheer force of his will to swallow this dose of democracy like the brave and obedient men they had sworn to be. But Spain was not to be spared pre-electoral violence. Terrorists struck between May 12 and 14, and six people were killed in the ongoing campaign to undermine the Juan Carlos–Suárez collaboration, provoke the army to revolt, (thus fulfilling prophecy that the military would not tolerate free elections), and, if elections nevertheless took place as scheduled, to strike enough fear into the voters to keep them away from the polls.

On June 15, 1977, the Spaniards voted, 18,447,714 of them, over 79 percent of the electorate. No party won the absolute majority of either the votes or of the seats in the new 350-member lower house, the Congress. (The upper house was named the Senate, and the two bodies together constituted the Cortes.) A voting system of proportional representation gave the centrist coalition, the Unión del Centro Democrático (UCD, Democratic Center Union), 34.8 percent of the votes and 165 seats; the Socialist party, Partido Socialista Obrero Español (PSOE, Spanish Socialist Worker's Party), 29.4 percent and 118 seats; the Communist party, Partido Comunista Español (PCE, Spanish Communist Party), 9.3 percent and 20 seats; the Conservative Coalition, Alianza Popular (AP, Popular Alliance), 8.4 percent and 16 seats; the Catalan party, Convergencia i Unio (CiU, Convergence and Union), 3.7 percent and 11 seats; and the Basque regionalist party, Partido Nacionalista Vasco (PNV, Basque Nationalist

Party), 1.7 percent and 8 seats. At the beginning of the campaign, 161 parties had been legalized, and more were legalized between the opening of the campaign and the elections. By election time, however, the number of parties had shrunk. Some had disappeared for lack of support. Some had been so small that Spanish wags said their membership could fit into two taxi cabs. Some had joined federations, hoping to increase their chances of success. The UCD was a federation of about a dozen parties whose members were Social Democrats, Christian Democrats, and Liberals of various hues. The union was dominated by Suárez, who had held the nation in suspense about his own candidacy until early May. The Alianza Popular was a conservative federation created by Manuel Fraga Iribarne from half a dozen right-wing (but not reactionary) political groups.

What did the elections reveal about Spanish politics and society eighteen months after Franco's death? The biggest surprise was the poor showing of the Communist party. Perhaps the enthusiasm for its legalization had been misread as enthusiasm for the party that had so carefully cultivated its mystique as the bravest and strongest opponent of Francoism. Possible reasons for the Communists' electoral weakness are discussed in Chapter 9. A second surprise was the total annihilation of those Christian Democrats who had chosen not to affiliate with the UCD and had opted instead to present themselves at the polls as a single party. In a Latin nation so overwhelmingly Catholic, in whose history the church had played so dominant a role, a confessional party would be expected to fare well, yet the election results indicated that unalloyed confessionalism was dead. (The Christian Democrats within the larger federation had a relatively healthy political future, however.) The extreme right seemed equally dead electorally; its federation, the Unión Nacional (UN, National Union), won but a single seat in Congress. The plight of the Communists, the Christian Democrats, and the extreme right confirms the relative moderation of the Spanish people, who voted instead for the UCD and the PSOE. This author calls the Socialists moderate even at this juncture. The party was still officially republican and Marxist (an adjective it would drop in less than two years), but its leader, Felipe González, had already demonstrated the consensuality that would soon characterize the party as well.

The moderation of the Spaniards should have come as little surprise to those who had been following the poll results published with great regularity since shortly before Franco's death. Pollsters asked the Spanish people about their politics, religion, jobs, income, and political philosophy; about their concerns and their contentment; and about their opinions on domestic and international affairs and the personalities involved in them. Much of this information may be found in the massive study, *Informe sociológico sobre el cambio político en España, 1975-1981,* published by the Fundación Foessa, whose surveys revealed in 1975 a reform-minded but far from desperate or radical people. Turning statistics into prose, the report states:

> Although the image of a society divided into classes continues to be predominant, we do not find a society in conflict or suffering social tension. Only 17 percent perceive society to be composed of classes in confrontation. Reformist aspirations and social demands have been produced in a climate of opinion moderated by the following factors: a) private economic conditions that have reached levels of well-being no one expects to be lowered in the future; b) an acceptance by the majority of the sanctity of personal, private property and its use by the family, although not necessarily its full use by the owners of the means of production; c) preservation of the conventional familial roles of authority; d) an acceptance of the principle of equality of opportunity, and not of the principle of absolute equality, operating in an environment of social mobility which militates against conflictual tensions.[2]

The election produced a modified Left-Right split, with the Right dominated by the center-right UCD, flanked by more extreme parties to its right, and the Left dominated by the center-left PSOE, flanked by more extreme parties to its left. Together, the two major parties gathered almost two-thirds of the popular vote. The UCD became the largest party in the Congress, but it did not have the absolute majority. It formed a minority government, rejecting coalition. The PSOE, as the second largest party, could thwart any program the UCD put forth if the Socialists allied themselves in opposition with other out parties. Some form of consensus—another of the catchwords of the transition—was necessary if the constitution writers were to succeed, and the congressional committee set up to draft the constitution was a compromise, reflective of the fundamental moderation revealed in the Foessa report. It included members of the UCD, the PSOE, the PCE, the PNV, and the AP.

It was to the enormous benefit of Spain that no party was sufficiently strong to hand down a constitution reflecting exclusively one political philosophy. Had the elections given one party or a group of like parties an absolute mandate, or had a bare electoral majority given the victors an exaggerated sense of mission, Spain might have suffered again as it did in 1931, when a constitution created by a zealous left ignored the wishes of a large minority of the population, which eventually rebelled in 1936.

COMPROMISE AND CONSENSUS

One must not forget that while the government and the Cortes were working to create the constitution for a new political order, they also had to operate the existing Francoist system until that new order dawned. The problems of state and society would not wait, yet long-range solutions could not be attempted until after the new constitution was approved. In the meantime, socioeconomic difficulties—especially inflation and unemployment—had to be faced. To do this with as little conflict as possible the government sought to pursue in the outside world the consensus forged inside the Cortes. The most significant success in that endeavor was the Moncloa Pacts (named for the residence and office of the prime minister) of October 1977.[3] The agreements, binding for two years, were negotiated in the Cortes among the leaders of the major political parties, in addition to the minority Basque and Catalan parties. Perhaps nothing could better illustrate the consensual nature of the pacts than the Socialists' and Communists' agreement to try to solve economic problems within the existing capitalist system. It was agreed that essential economic reform would be brought about within the existing market economy, distributing the burdens of adjustment equally among the various societal groups. Among other things, the pact called for a ceiling on wage increases; a restructuring of public expenditures, including social security; restrictions on credit; tax reform; price controls on essential commodities; effective unemployment insurance; efforts to retrain the unemployed and to increase job opportunities; and fiscal and financial reform. In addition to the economic revisions, sociopolitical reforms were urged as well, among them the decriminalization of adultery, the legalization of contraceptives, and the modification of rape statutes (all of particular interest to women), and the reorganization of the police and of the military Civil Guard and Armed Police.

In their efforts to conciliate the legitimate grievances of those provinces that had suffered so long under Madrid's heavy hand and to make the national environment as congenial as possible for the gestation and birth of the constitution, Suárez and the king began to recognize regional demands. In September 1977 a pre-autonomy decree was issued for Catalonia, reestablishing the Generalitat, the local regional legislature first created during the Second Republic. In December 1977, a pre-autonomy decree was issued for the Basque provinces of Álava, Guipúzcoa, and Vizcaya. Navarre, the fourth Basque province, which chose not to be in league with the other three, was given separate treatment. Autonomy would have to wait until the provisions of the new constitution went into effect, but these early actions ensured that when the constitution was ratified, the three Basque provinces and Catalonia, the regions that had endured the harshest repression under Franco, would be the first to enjoy autonomy. The Navarrese had fought with Franco during the Civil War and thus earned his devotion, not his emnity.

The pre-autonomy decrees did not stop here. Once autonomy had been accepted as legitimate for Catalonia and the Basque lands, the rest of Spain quickly voiced its own demands. Galicia had a claim almost as special as Catalonia and the Basque territories, based primarily on a separate language and culture. A pre-autonomy decree went out to Galicia in March 1978, and at the same time to Valencia, Aragon, and the Canary Islands. In April 1978, Andalucia, the Balearic Islands, Extremadura, and Old Castile–Leon received pre-autonomy decrees; in August, Murcia and Asturias, and in September, New Castile–La Mancha.

In the Congress, the constitution was drafted by a 7-member subcommittee of the 36-member Committee on Constitutional Affairs. On the main committee were 17 members of the UCD, 13 Socialists, 2 Communists, 2 members of the AP, 1 Catalan, and 1 Basque. On the subcommittee were 3 members of the UCD, 1 Socialist, 1 Communist, 1 member of the AP, and 1 Catalan. Had the members of the main committee foreseen the problems that the Basques within the Congress would cause later, perhaps they would have substituted a Basque for a Catalan on the subcommittee, or included both.

The consensus that produced the main committee and subcommittee memberships prevailed, more or less, during the first drafting of the document finished by mid-November 1977. Consensuality, aided by the strict secrecy that surrounded the research and writing of the articles, was dealt a blow when part of the first draft was leaked to a magazine and published. A few days later the entire first draft was published without authorization in a Madrid newspaper. A second draft was then presented to the main committee for full debate in mid-December following the unplanned public airing that resulted from the leaks. By early January over 1,000 amendments had been proposed to the second draft, which then went back to the subcommittee for additional work. By now consensuality was under severe strain, for even moderate men may fall out when sensitive issues are discussed in public, and not all members of the main committee or subcommittee were moderates or representatives of moderates. The Basques and some Catalans, for example, remained obdurate to the bitter end, and many issues were undeniably explosive: regional autonomy, the place of the Catholic church in the new system, state aid to private schools (almost all of them Catholic), abortion, divorce, and the right of employers to use the lockout.

More significant than the inflexibility of the Basques and a few Catalans were the confrontations between the two major parties, the UCD and the PSOE, which were approaching an impasse. The solution that broke the impending deadlock demonstrated the reality of power and how it was used at this stage of the transition. Prime Minister Suárez and Felipe González, after Suárez the most powerful politician in Spain, instructed their seconds-in-command to find a solution to the stalemate out of the glare of publicity. In typical Spanish fashion, they did so sitting over a table in a Madrid restaurant. They worked throughout the night of May 28, 1978, reaching agreement about dawn the next day. From that point on, the full committee's approval of the draft was assured, even though there would be more debate and the representatives of the minor parties would protest furiously at what they saw as railroading by the two major parties.

Debate on the floors of the Congress and the Senate took place from July 4, 1978, to October 5, 1978, and after a joint committee reconciled the differences between the drafts as they emerged from the two houses of the Cortes, the final vote was taken on October 31, 1978. The long and detailed finished document contained 169 articles and 15,000 words. Of the 350 members of the Congress, 345 were present for the vote: 325 representatives, including all except 1 of the Catalans, voted "yes"; the "no" votes came primarily from the Basques and 5 members of the AP. Of the 248 members of the Senate, 239 voted "yes," the "no" votes coming from the Basques and the Catalans.

The constitution was ratified by the Spanish in the referendum held on December 6, 1978. The response of the electorate was not overwhelming, but there was approval by an absolute majority. The percentage of the electorate who voted in the constitutional referendum of 1978 was far smaller than the number that had initiated the systemic restructuring in 1976 with the referendum approving the Law for Political Change. In the 1976 referendum, 16,573,180 citizens voted "yes" out of 17,599,662 who went to the polls, from a total electorate of 22,644,290. In other words, 73.2 percent of the eligible voters cast "yes" ballots. In the referendum of 1978, out of the 17,873,301 votes cast, 15,706,078 voted "yes" and only 1,400,505 voted "no," but there were 8,755,879 abstentions. The "yes" vote was 87.87 percent of all those voting, but only 59.87 percent of the total electorate went to the polls. John Coverdale offered the following analysis:

> The degree of approval was, however, impressive for three reasons: this was the third time Spaniards had been called to the polls in two years; it was widely believed that the constitution would be easily approved and that, therefore, there was little need to vote; and a detailed text was bound to alienate more people than a general proposal for democratic reform like that presented two years earlier.[4]

The constitution was sanctioned by King Juan Carlos I in the presence of the Cortes on December 27, 1978, and published in the *Boletín Oficial del Estado* (Official Bulletin of the State) on December 29, 1978, entering in force as of that date.

NOTES

1. Raymond Carr and Juan Pablo Fusi, *Spain: Dictatorship to Democracy*, 2d ed. (London: George Allen and Unwin, 1981), p. 191.

2. *Informe sociológico sobre el cambio político en España, 1975–1981* (Madrid: Editorial Euramérica, S.A., 1981), pp. 8–9.

3. Servicio Central de Publicaciones, *Los Pactos de Moncloa*, Collección Informe No. 17 (Madrid: 1977).

4. John Coverdale, *The Political Transformation of Spain after Franco* (New York: Praeger, 1979), p. 119.

7

The Constitution

The constitution ratified by the Spaniards on December 6, 1978, is their ninth since the promulgation of the great liberal constitution written in Cádiz in 1812 during the Peninsular War against Napoleon and before the restoration of the Bourbons two years later.[1] Constitutions that became operative were created in 1812, 1834, 1837, 1845, 1869, 1876, 1931, and 1938–1967 (the years during which Franco produced the seven Fundamental Laws that together made up his "constitution"). The list does not include two constitutions that never became active (1808 and 1856) nor two that never got off the drawing board (1852 and 1873). Most of the constitutions listed above were not the expression of the popular will but were imposed from above, yet their number alone gives evidence of the precarious and ephemeral nature of the Spanish constitutional experience.

Why should one expect that the fate of the constitution of 1978 might be different from that of the other eight and that the Spaniards might finally be able to enjoy constitutional longevity and stability? The answer in part lies in the knowledge that the document was produced by a constituent assembly elected by the people and ratified by popular referendum. It also lies in the knowledge that for the first time in their history the Spaniards have a political system that is more or less congruent with their socioeconomic system, which, according to Harry Eckstein, is essential to efficiency and stability. Popular experiences in the major public arenas—economic, social, and political—are becoming reinforcing rather than antagonistic, and thus the Spaniards are creating systemic

109

supports that grow tighter and stronger each day. The constitutional commentators Jorge de Esteban and Luis López Guerra wrote that the new constitution is democratic, bourgeois, and progressive because Spaniards are now democratic, bourgeois, and progressive. Of course, the Spaniards also wrote and approved their own document in 1931 when they created the Second Republic, but the major arenas in Spanish society in 1931 were highly incongruent and mutually destructive, and the republic was doomed from the very beginning, as hindsight has shown.

The 1978 constitution (see excerpts in the appendix to this chapter) is a modern, post–World War II document largely inspired by the Italian constitution of 1947 and the German Basic Law of 1949. It lays equal emphasis on the social and the individualistic nature of human beings, with the realization that winning political freedom unaccompanied by social and economic liberation is a hollow achievement. At the same time, the 1978 constitution is a classic nineteenth-century document, with its catalog of individual rights and its insistence on the equitable distribution of power between the executive and legislative functions, even though the modern reality of powerful executive initiative is clearly accommodated. The document does not go nearly as far as the constitution of the French Fifth Republic, which shifts the balance unequivocally toward the executive. Perhaps a copy of the French model would have made better sense given the way politics works today, but the experience of Franco is so fresh and so painful to so many that an emphasis on executive power would not have been tolerated by most Spaniards.

RIGHTS AND FREEDOMS

The Spaniards are keenly aware of the political rights they were deprived of for almost forty years, and the constitution lists in detail those values they consider to be sacred, emphasizing four inalienable rights: liberty, justice, equality, and the right to freely express oneself politically. Within a collective spirit, democracy guarantees the individual's political rights, and equality gives every citizen's vote and political presence the same weight as everyone else's. Moreover, the citizen may join the political party and the groups of his or her choice, provided that the organizations are structured democratically and respect the constitution. Most of the post-war European constitutions contain guarantees spelling out the indispensability of political parties and groups to the democratic process (guarantees not found in the classic nine-teenth-century documents), and in that regard articles 6 and 22 in the Spanish constitution resemble article 4 in the French constitution and article 21 in the German Basic Law. Although all political groups are protected in article 22, labor and management groups receive special mention in article 7 of the Spanish constitution, so that there might be no doubt about their legality. The constitution speaks of the groups of both labor and management, but the article was designed primarily to protect labor, which had suffered worse repression under Franco than probably any other group. Even the liberal upper class professions had suffered severe restrictions under Franco, and their associations also receive special attention in article 36 of the 1978 constitution.

In addition to the right to join groups and parties, the Spaniard can participate in the political process in several ways. Article 23 guarantees the right to elect political representatives either directly or indirectly. Article 27 instructs the legislature to receive written individual or collective petitions. Popular initiative, with certain restrictions, is set forth in article 87, which stipulates that a minimum of 500,000 accredited signatures may set in motion the national legislative process. Finally, the people are to be consulted in referenda, compulsory for constitutional amendment or revision (article 168), discretionary for a prime minister seeking support for particularly sensitive issues. American readers may be especially interested in the provisions for the initiative and the referendum, neither of which is constitutional at the national level in the United States. Meaningful positive and negative arguments can be made about the political safety of such devices within a basically representative system like the Spanish, but it is undeniable that both the initiative and the referendum allow citizens an additional voice in the process, irrespective of how wisely or foolishly it may be used. A people like the Spanish, so long deprived of any voice at all, are obviously willing to run the demagogic risk inherent in direct democracy.

The Spanish constitution includes rights also found in the constitutions of the oldest democratic societies; other rights commonly found in ordinary law or judicial interpretation in these older democracies have been constitutionalized in Spain. Perhaps the constitution should not have been burdened thus, particularly as so many of these statements are quite vague, but once again, the spectre of the immediate past compelled the founders of the new regime to make fast as many protections as possible by securing them on paper at least. Freedom of conscience (article 16); freedom of expression, especially freedom from prior censorship (article 20); freedom of peaceful reunion without prior permission (article 21); freedom of association (article 22); and freedom of religion (article 16) are classic liberal civil rights. Freedom of religion posed problems to the writers of the Spanish constitution. Catholicism is the religion of almost all Spaniards, even if most no longer practice it with regularity. The Catholic church had a special place of honor and power in Franco's Spain, and in the eyes of many Spaniards its image was badly tarnished. Yet the universality of the church in Spain (the non-Catholic population is infinitesimal) could not be gainsaid, and Catholicism was given honorable mention in the article recognizing freedom of religion and establishing a secular state. "There will be no state church. The public authorities will be aware of the religious beliefs of the Spanish people and will maintain relations of cooperation with the Catholic church and all other religions."[2]

Beyond the general guarantees of freedom of association found in article 22, the right of workers to organize into unions is spelled out very specifically in article 28, which treats labor as a special category and guarantees that everyone has the right not only to join unions (with certain restrictions applying to civil servants) but also to strike.

SOCIAL COMMITMENTS

Along with the newly constitutionalized right to strike, several other rights rarely found in older constitutions have also been enshrined in the Spanish document. Most of them are to be implemented by organic laws yet to be passed. As they read now, they represent little more than future commitments, consummations devoutly to be wished, and embody the social nature of the new Spanish state. Article 43 recognizes the right of each person to health protection, almost the right to good health. Article 47 states that all Spaniards have the right to enjoy decent housing, and article 44 obligates the public authorities to provide all Spaniards access to culture. Children, whether legitimate or not (article 44); adolescents (article 48); and the elderly, called the "third age" in the Spanish constitution (article 50), are singled out for special concern, as are the mentally, physically, and sensorally handicapped (article 49). The constitution appears most daring from a societal point of view by protecting the family (article 39) without stating that the family emerges from matrimony, whose free contract is honored in article 32. For what historically has been a conservative, Catholic society this ambiguity, which could not have been an oversight, reveals a new spirit made even more manifest in article 32, which speaks about the possibility of separation and the dissolution of marriage. This position on divorce is revolutionary; nothing could have been more heinous under the Franco regime or even before.

Because a national network of state schools—albeit of uneven quality—is already in place, the most immediate realizable of the social rights to be enjoyed by Spaniards is the right to a basic education, which is both obligatory and free (article 27). The article contains ambiguous guarantees that could not have been avoided. The relationship between church and state in regard to education was among the most sensitive issues to confront the drafters of the constitution. Pressure from the church hierarchy, and from the laity for whom access to Catholic education was as sacred as access to the sacraments, was overwhelming. The Catholic church, and by extension its institutions, had already been singled out for particular consideration in article 16. The numerous Catholic primary and secondary schools throughout the country educate a large percentage of Spanish children, particularly from among the elite, and these were subventioned during the Franco regime. The constitution provides in article 27 that the public authorities guarantee the right possessed by parents to have their children receive the moral and religious training that is appropriate to the family's convictions. Does this mean that religious education should be financially assisted? What manner of support would be provided, and for what kinds of education? For special classes within the state school system? For separate schools for religious study? For religiously affiliated schools that offer the gamut of basic education? Moreover, would all religious instruction be aided, or only Catholic instruction? Of the limited resources available, must the public funds earmarked for state institutions be divided among nonstate educational institutions, possibly lowering the quality of state education? These potentially explosive questions remained to be answered.

The guarantees that make up the state's social commitments are for the most part imprecise. Some social commitments are more conclusive, however, and in a nonpejorative sense, more radical. Article 33 recognizes the right to inheritance and to private property but qualifies the right by the warning that the social function of property and inheritance limits their private usage. Private property is not an inalienable right; it is denied legal preeminence and sanctity. Enlarging the limitations on private property (and by extension on private business operated according to the dictates of its owners or shareholders), article 129 establishes the constitutionality of worker participation in and access to the property of the means of production. Even though this article awaits elaboration by future law, it outlines definite rights, constitutionalizing a function and not merely a commitment.

As we have already seen, the constitution ensures the worker's right to unionize, and to strike, and to bargain collectively with management (articles 28, 24). Moreover, it recognizes the worker's need for assistance when misfortune hits, particularly unemployment, and establishes social security for all citizens (article 41). The constitution also indulges in devout wishes, stating that all Spaniards have not only the duty but also the right to work (article 35), giving the impression that the state is obligated to provide a job for everyone. Yet if this obligation were binding, would it not obviate the necessity for the unemployment compensation guaranteed in article 41? Perhaps the intention was not to guarantee all Spaniards a job but to guarantee that no one who wanted to work would be deprived arbitrarily of the opportunity to do so.

The constitutionality of the state's intervention in the economic process is set forth in article 128, which also declares that the use of all resources of the country in all forms is subordinate to the general interest. Moreover, in article 40 the state is empowered to further social and economic progress and bring about a fairer distribution of both personal and regional income, if necessary through planning by the state with the aid and collaboration of both private and public economic organizations (article 131).

Is this a socialist constitution? No, because individual rights are firmly secured, but as de Esteban and López Guerra phrase it: "We are not faced with a socialist model but one which is 'socializable.'"[3] The same authors conclude: "It is a socially progressive constitution in that it permits action by the public authorities (particularly legislative action) in conformity with economic and social principles which suppose a considerable transformation of social reality."[4] The vague and imprecise aspirations signify, if not the opening of clear paths to the future, at least the closing of paths that would take society back to the past.

NOTES

1. *Constitución Española* (Madrid: Boletín Oficial del Estado, 1981).

2. Ibid., article 16 (translation by author).

3. Jorge de Esteban and Luis López Guerra, *El régimen constitucional Español,* 2 vols. (Barcelona: Labor Universitaria, 1982), p. 338.

4. Ibid., p. 348.

Appendix
Excerpts from the Constitution

Preliminary Title

Art. 1. (1) Spain constitutes a social and democratic state of law, advocating as higher values of its legal order liberty, justice, equality and political pluralism.

(2) National sovereignty is vested in the Spanish people from whom emanate the powers of the state.

(3) The political form of the Spanish state is that of parliamentary monarchy.

Art. 2. The Constitution is based on the indissoluble unity of the Spanish nation, the common and indivisible country of all Spaniards, and recognizes and guarantees the right to self-government of the nationalities and regions of which it is composed and solidarity among them all.

Art. 6. The political parties are the expression of political pluralism, co-operate in the formation and expression of the will of the people and are a basic instrument for political participation. Their creation and the exercise of their activity are free in so far as they are compatible with respect for the Constitution and the law. Their internal structure and operation must be democratic.

Art. 7. Trade unions and employers' associations contribute to the defence and promotion of the economic and social interests proper to them. Their creation and the exercise of their activity are free in so far as they are compatible with respect for the Constitution and the law. Their internal structure and operation must be democratic.

Title I.—Concerning Fundamental Rights and Duties

Art. 10. (1) Human dignity, man's inviolable and inherent rights, the free development of his personality, respect for the law and for the rights of others are fundamental to political order and social peace.

(2) The standards relative to the fundamental rights and liberties recognized by the Constitution shall be interpreted in conformity with the [1948] Universal Declaration of Human Rights [ratified by Spain on April 27, 1977] and the international treaties and agreements thereon ratified by Spain.

Art. 14. Spaniards are equal before the law and may not in any way be discriminated against on account of birth, race, sex, religion, opinion or any other condition or personal or social circumstance.

Art. 15. Every person has the right to life and physical and moral integrity, and may under no circumstances be subject to torture or to inhuman or degrading punishment or treatment. The death penalty shall be abolished, except as provided by any military criminal law in wartime.

Art. 16. (1) Freedom of ideology, religion and worship of individuals and communities is guaranteed, with no more restrictions on their expression than may be necessary in order to maintain the public order protected by law.

(2) Nobody may be compelled to make declarations regarding his religion, beliefs or ideologies.

(3) There shall be no state religion. The public authorities shall take the religious beliefs of Spanish society into account and shall maintain the consequent relations of co-operation with the Catholic Church and the other confessions.

Art. 23. (1) Citizens have the right to participate in public affairs, directly or through their representatives freely elected in periodic elections by universal suffrage.

Art. 27. (1) Everyone is entitled to education. Freedom of instruction is recognized.

(2) Education shall have as its objective the full development of the human personality compatible with respect for the democratic principles of coexistence and for the fundamental rights and liberties.

(3) The public authorities guarantee the right of parents to ensure that their children receive religious and moral instruction compatible with their own convictions.

(4) Basic education is compulsory and free of charge.

(5) The public authorities guarantee the right of everyone to education, through general planning of education, with the effective participation of all parties concerned and the setting up of teaching establishments.

(6) The right of individuals and legal entities to set up teaching establishments is recognized, provided they are compatible with respect for constitutional principles.

(7) Teachers, parents and, when appropriate, pupils shall participate in the control and management of all the centres maintained by the administration with public funds, under the terms to be laid down by the law.

(8) The public authorities shall inspect and standardize the education system in order to guarantee compliance with the law.

(9) The public authorities shall help teaching establishments which meet the requirements to be laid down by the law.

(10) The autonomy of the universities is recognized, under the terms to be laid down by the law.

Art. 28. (1) Everyone has the right freely to join a trade union. The law may limit the exercise of this right or make an exception to it in the case of the armed forces or institutes or other corps subject to military discipline, and shall regulate the special features of its exercise by public officials. Trade union freedom includes the right to found trade unions and to join the union of one's choice, as well as the right of the trade unions to form confederations and found international trade union organizations, or to become members of same. Nobody may be compelled to join a trade union.

(2) The right of workers to strike in defence of their interests is recognized. The law regulating the exercise of this right shall establish the guarantees necessary to ensure the maintenance of essential community services.

Art. 35. (1) All Spaniards have the duty to work and the right to employment, to free choice of profession or trade, to advancement through their work, and to sufficient remuneration for the satisfaction of their needs and those of their families, while in no case may they be discriminated against on account of their sex.

(2) The law shall establish a workers' statute.

Art. 38. Free enterprise is recognized within the framework of a market economy. The public authorities shall guarantee and protect its exercise and the safeguarding of productivity in accordance with the demands of the economy in general and, as the case may be, of its planning.

Title II.—Concerning the Crown

Art. 56. (1) The King is the head of state, the symbol of its unity and permanence. He arbitrates and moderates the regular working of the institutions, assumes the highest representation of the Spanish state in international relations, especially with those nations belonging to the same historic community, and exercises the functions expressly conferred on him by the Constitution and the law.

(2) His title is King of Spain, and he may use the other titles belonging to the Crown.

(3) The person of the King is inviolable and is not subject to liability. His acts shall always be countersigned in the manner established in Article 64. Without such countersignature they shall lack validity, except as provided for in Article 65 (2).

Art. 62. It is incumbent upon the King:

(a) to sanction and promulgate the laws;

(b) to summon and dissolve the *Cortes Generales* and to call elections upon the terms provided for in the Constitution;

(c) to call a referendum in the cases provided for in the Constitution;

(d) to propose a candidate for President of the Government [Prime Minister] and, as the case may be, appoint him or remove him from office, under the terms provided in the Constitution;

(e) to appoint and dismiss members of the Government at the proposal of its President;

(f) to issue the decrees agreed upon by the Council of Ministers, to confer civil and military employment and award honours and distinctions in conformity with the law;

(g) to keep himself informed about the affairs of state and to preside, for this purpose, over the meetings of the Councils of Ministers when he deems opportune, at the request of the President of the Government;

(h) to exercise supreme command of the armed forces;

(i) to exercise the right to grant pardons in accordance with the law, which may not authorize general pardons;

(j) to exercise the high patronage of the royal academies.

Art. 63. (1) The King accredits ambassadors and other diplomatic representatives. Foreign representatives in Spain are accredited to him.

(2) It is incumbent on the King to express the state's assent to make international commitments through treaties, in conformity with the Constitution and the law.

(3) It is incumbent on the King, following authorization by the *Cortes Generales*, to declare war and make peace.

Art. 64. (1) The King's acts shall be countersigned by the President of the Government and, where appropriate, by the competent ministers. The nomination and appointment of the President of the Government, and the dissolution provided for in Article 99 shall be countersigned by the President of the Congress [of Deputies].

(2) Those countersigning the King's acts shall be liable for them.

Title III.—Concerning the Cortes Generales

Art. 66. (1) The *Cortes Generales* represent the Spanish people and consist of the Congress of Deputies and the Senate.

(2) The *Cortes Generales* exercise the legislative power of the state, approve its budgets, control government action and hold all the other powers vested in them by the Constitution.

(3) The *Cortes Generales* are inviolable.

Art. 68. (1) Congress consists of a minimum of 300 and a maximum of 400 deputies, elected by universal, free, equal, direct and secret suffrage on the terms laid down by the law.

(2) The electoral district is the province. The cities of Ceuta and Melilla shall each be represented by a deputy. The total number of deputies shall be distributed in accordance with the law, each electoral district being assigned a minimum initial representation and the rest being distributed in proportion to the population.

(3) The election in each electoral district shall be conducted on the basis of proportional representation.

(4) Congress is elected for four years. The term of office of the deputies ends four years after their election or on the day that the chamber is dissolved.

(5) All Spaniards who are entitled to the full exercise of their political rights are electors and eligible for election.

The law shall recognize and the state shall facilitate the exercise of the right of suffrage of Spaniards who find themselves outside Spanish territory.

(6) Elections shall take place between 30 and 60 days after the end of the term of office. Congress-elect must be summoned within 25 days after the holding of elections.

Title V.—Concerning the Relations Between the Government and the Cortes Generales

Art. 108. The Government is jointly answerable to the Congress of Deputies for its political management.

Art. 112. The President of the Government, after deliberation by the Council of Ministers, may ask Congress for a vote of confidence in favour of his programme or of a general policy statement. Confidence shall be considered obtained when a simple majority of the deputies votes in favour.

Art. 113. (1) The Congress of Deputies may challenge government policy by means of the adoption by an absolute majority of its members of a motion of censure..

(2) The motion of censure must be proposed by at least one-tenth of the deputies, including a candidate for the office of President of the Government.

(3) The motion of censure may not be voted until five days after it has been submitted. During the first two days of this period, alternative motions may be submitted.

(4) If the motion of censure is not passed by Congress, its signatories may not submit another during the same session.

Art. 114. (1) If Congress withholds its confidence from the Government, the latter shall submit its resignation to the King, whereafter a President of the Government shall be nominated in accordance with the provisions of Article 99.

(2) If Congress adopts a motion of censure, the Government shall submit its resignation to the King, while the candidate proposed in the motion of censure shall be considered to have the confidence of the chambers for the purposes provided in Article 99. The King shall appoint him President of the Government.

Art. 115. (1) The President of the Government, after deliberation by the Council of Ministers, and under his own exclusive responsibility, may propose the dissolution of the Congress, the Senate or the *Cortes Generales*, which shall be decreed by the King. The decree of dissolution shall set the date of the election.

(2) The proposal for dissolution may not be submitted while a motion for censure is in process.

(3) There shall be no further dissolution until a year has elapsed since the previous one, except as provided for in Article 99, Clause (5).

Title VII.—*Economy and Finance*

Art. 128. (1) All the wealth of the country in its different forms, by whomsoever it may be owned, is subordinate to the general interest.

(2) Public initiative in economic activity is recognized. Essential resources or services may be restricted by law to the public sector, especially in the case of monopolies. Likewise, intervention in companies may be decided upon when the public interest so demands.

Art. 143. (1) In the exercise of the right to self-government recognized in Article 2 of the Constitution, bordering provinces with common historic, cultural and economic characteristics, island territories and provinces with historic regional status may accede to self-government and form self-governing communities in conformity with the provisions contained in this Title and in the respective statutes.

(2) The right to initiate the process towards self-government [hereinafter referred to as "the initiative towards self-government" or "the initiative"] lies with all the provincial councils concerned or with the corresponding inter-island body and with two-thirds of the municipalities whose populations represent at least the majority of the electorate of each province or island. These requirements must be met within six months from the initial agreement adopted to this effect by any of the local corporations concerned.

(3) If this initiative should not be successful, it may only be repeated after five years have elapsed.

Art. 151. (1) It shall not be necessary to wait for the five-year period referred to in Clause (2) of Article 148 to elapse when the initiative for attaining self-government is agreed upon within the time limit specified in Article 143, Clause (2), not only by the corresponding provincial councils or inter-island bodies but also by three-quarters of the municipalities of each province concerned, representing at least the majority of the electorate of each one, and the said initiative is ratified in a referendum by the absolute majority of the electors in each province, under the terms to be laid down by an organic law.

(*Source: Keesing's Contemporary Archives*, Oct. 5, 1979. Reprinted by permission of the copyright holder, Longman Group Ltd., Harlow, Essex, U.K.)

8

The Political System

Spain is a constitutional monarchy with a parliamentary government in the form of a bicameral legislature. The state is unitary and indivisible, but the constitution recognizes the creation of autonomous regions within the state. These regions are forbidden to federate with one another, and their power and authority emerge from the constitution and remain subject to it. In other words, no region, irrespective of its history and its preeminence, may claim that the right to autonomy predates the constitution. All political rights in Spain today were born with the constitution of 1978.

THE MONARCHY

Juan Carlos I is the first monarch of the new Spanish polity, and his status arises exclusively from the constitution. Yet at the same time he is the recognized descendant of the historic Bourbon house, whose continuity was broken by the Second Republic in 1931. After 1936 the house was restored in name only by Franco, who ruled absolutely and single-handedly for thirty-nine years with no monarch present on Spanish soil. Franco decreed that Spain had never ceased being a monarchy, on the valid basis that Alfonso XIII had never officially abdicated in 1931 but had instead only gone into exile. Franco chose Juan Carlos, the grandson of Alfonso XIII, as his successor, though Alfonso's son, Don Juan de Borbón, was (and is) still alive. Don Juan has now sworn allegiance to his son and thus no longer maintains a claim to the throne. Is Juan Carlos king of Spain because of heredity, because of Franco, or because of the constitution of 1978? He is king for all three reasons and thus occupies a unique position. The next king or queen of Spain will reign only because of the constitution, even though he or she will ascend to the throne as the heir of the first king of the new regime, Juan Carlos I. Juan Carlos can also be seen as the last king of the old regime, whether the old regime is interpreted to be that of Franco or that of the Bourbons.

The complex position of Juan Carlos I serves both to maintain continuity and to break it at the same time, to change Spain fundamentally politically while leaving the centerpiece, the king, untouched. To repudiate the new democratic regime one must repudiate Juan Carlos, and hence both the legacy of Franco, whose heir he is, and the Bourbon dynasty. To accept Juan Carlos, one accepts the new democratic constitution that established him. Those loyal to Franco, the Bourbons, or both—particularly the extreme Right and the military—could not extricate themselves from this dilemma, which situation has contributed mightily to the stability of the fledgling political system.

Under the constitution the monarch's sole political power is to nominate candidates for the prime ministership, but even this power is severely limited when a single party has a clear majority in Congress, the lower house of the legislature, making that party's candidate the inevitable choice. Only when coalitions are unavoidable does the king's power come into play. Apart from this, the king symbolizes the unity and permanence of the state and arbitrates and moderates the functioning of its institutions (article 56). But he does not possess a reserve of power above the state as the president of France appears to, nor does the Spanish king possess emergency powers. The Spanish king resembles instead the British monarch, who, as British historian Walter Bagehot has said, warns, advises, and may be consulted. The Spanish sovereign differs from the British, however, in that Juan Carlos does not embody the totality of power—a British fiction that maintains that every political function is Her Majesty's function and every public institution is Her Majesty's institution. Custom and tradition play no role in the Spanish sovereign's power, delimiting or expanding it by a universal understanding of the rules of the game. Article 62 specifically enumerates the powers of the monarch, all of whose political acts must be countersigned by a minister or by the president of the Congress. Even though it is the monarch alone who sanctions and promulgates the law, practical reality would make it impossible for him to refuse his signature. If a monarch were to act in a manner deemed unconstitutional, he or she could be declared incapacitated by the Cortes under article 59 and removed from the throne.

What the king possesses uncontestably is authority, and Juan Carlos is building this quality strongly and wisely, setting precedents from which his heirs, if they have any sense at all, will be able to profit. It is generally conceded that the transition to democracy from Francoism could not have taken place as smoothly as it did without Juan Carlos' deep commitment to democratic values and without his practical understanding of present-day politics. It may be that the experience of his brother-in-law, formerly King Constantine of Greece, showed the Spanish king what to avoid. Whatever his motivations, Juan Carlos has performed the royal role superbly, making himself almost indispensable as the source of wisdom and moderation to be consulted at every crucial step in the political process. As we shall see later in this study, his behavior at the time of the attempted coup d'état in February 1981 is credited with saving the regime.

GOVERNMENTAL STRUCTURE

The government or cabinet is composed of the president (president of the government is the title of the prime minister in Spain); the vice-presidents, whose number is left unspecified in the constitution; and the ministers, whose number is also left unspecified (article 98). But the position that is of singular concern is that of the prime minister, who, once accepted by the Congress, has the exclusive power to form the government. The candidate for the presidential position is presented by the king to the Congress for approval. If one party has an absolute majority in the Congress, the king's choice, in practice if not in theory, would be limited to that party's leader. If there were no clear majority, the king's discretion would increase in proportion to the complexity of the party composition in the lower house, with the monarch freely choosing, even from outside the Congress, that man or woman who seemed capable of putting together a working coalition. If, on the first balloting, the Congress accepts the king's nominee by an absolute majority, the sovereign then proclaims the nominee prime minster. If an absolute majority is not obtained, the second balloting on the same candidate takes place forty-eight hours later, and the nominee becomes president of the government if he or she wins a simple majority (receiving more "yes" than "no" votes). If this majority is not reached, a new nominee is presented by the king. If after two months no candidate is able to win approval using the system described above, the king, with the approval of the president of the Congress (the equivalent of majority leader), dissolves both houses of the legislature and calls for new elections (article 99). Once approved, the prime minster is free to compose the cabinet as he or she sees fit with no further legislative approval, placing in it anyone that political reality permits. The prime minister may dismiss members of the cabinet with the same freedom, yet once formed, the cabinet, becomes a collegial body. No single minister or group of ministers may be removed by legislative action. The legislature may remove the prime minister, but when this occurs the entire cabinet goes too.

The constitution makes the tenure of the government very secure, however. The life of the cabinet (or more precisely that of the prime minister) is designed to last the four-year term of the Congress. The prime minister may be removed before that time only by an act of censure, which is difficult to execute. The procedure must be initiated by a petition signed by no fewer than 10 percent of all the deputies. The motion must include the name of the candidate who would replace the incumbent prime minister if the action were to succeed. If the attempt to censure fails, those deputies who signed the petition are foreclosed from initiating another motion during that legislative session. Voting by the Congress may take place no sooner than five days from the presentation of the motion, and during that time the candidate for the prime ministership (for whom a substitute may be made during the first two days) presents his or her program for debate. The censure is successful if it receives the approval of an absolute majority of deputies, following which the incumbent president of the government would resign and the king present the victorious candidate for approval.

A prime minster may attempt to strengthen his or her own position by calling for a vote of confidence in periods of stress or following a major shift in policy or a cabinet reshuffle. The success of the vote is measured by a simple majority of the deputies present, (more "yes" than "no" votes). Failure to receive that majority means that the prime minister and the entire cabinet must resign. The process of finding a new prime minister follows the pattern already described.

A prime minister may attempt to extend his mandate (and that of this party) by dissolving just Congress or both the Congress and the Senate, and calling for new elections. This weapon may not be used by the prime minister while a censure motion is in progress, nor may the weapon be used earlier than a year following the preceding motion (except in those cases in which, after two months, a new president of the government cannot be found in the event the one who dissolved the legislature is repudiated at the polls).

These devices strengthen the hand of the president of the government vis-à-vis the legislature, while protecting the latter's ultimate control of the political fate of the state. The prime minister's dominance is also felt in the legislative process, which gives bills originating with the government, *proyectos de ley,* priority over bills originating with the legislature, *proposiciones de ley* (article 89). The government has exclusive budgetary initiative, and any alteration in taxation or expenditures by the legislature must have prior governmental approval (article 134). This has been interpreted to mean that all budgetary proposals must come from the government, but may be amended by the legislature; once the budget has been approved, however, it may not subsequently be altered by the legislature without the permission of the cabinet.

The government may also pass decree laws in times of "urgent and extraordinary necessity" (article 86). These laws, put into operation at the government's discretion, are subject to several restrictions. A decree may touch neither the basic institutions of the state nor the basic civil rights of the people; a decree must be immediately submitted to the Congress for debate, which must take place during the thirty days following the decree's promulgation; Congress may accept or reject a decree or may treat it as if it were a governmental bill (*proyecto de ley*) and handle it as a matter of urgency (article 90).

THE LEGISLATURE

There are two houses in the legislature—the lower, called the Congress, and the upper, called the Senate. Together they constitute the Cortes. The Spanish constitution, typical of most post–World War II constitutions, limits the powers of the Senate. The Congress dominates the legislature, and the government is responsible solely to the lower house.

The size of the Congress is established in article 68, which sets the minimum number of deputies at 300 and the maximum at 400. The deputies are chosen for four years in the fifty provinces into which Spain is divided. All citizens eighteen years old and over enjoy free, equal, direct, and secret suffrage. Each province (plus Ceuta and Melilla, the city-states on the Moroccan coast that have been Spanish for centuries) is guaranteed a minimum of one deputy (which rewards the sparsely populated provinces), and the remaining seats are distributed among the provinces according to population. The provincial seats are then distributed by party in proportion to the number of votes each party receives. The key words are "by party," because the electoral system calls for closed and blocked ballots; citizens must vote a straight ticket and accept the order of the candidates as they appear on the ballot.

The size of the Senate is established in article 69. Each mainland province receives four senators (once again, sparsely settled provinces are rewarded); Ceuta and Melilla each receive two senators; and the two insular provinces (the Balearic Islands in the Mediterranean and the Canary Islands in the Atlantic) receive a total of sixteen. The Senators are elected for four years by citizens eighteen years old and over through free, equal, direct, and secret suffrage, but the constitution allows an organic law to determine how senators are to be chosen. At the present time, a majority system has been adopted, but this could be replaced in the future, as the electoral system is not constitutionally fixed. The Senate will also have representatives from the autonomous regions, and is in fact the forum for those regions. As each region achieves autonomy, it is guaranteed at least one senator plus one additional senator for every million inhabitants.

Each of the chambers of the legislature has a party structure, a president (majority leader), a *Mesa* (executive committee), a *Junta de Portavoces* (a board of party representatives), and a system of committees and subcommittees. Because of the condensed nature of this study, details will be given only for the more powerful Congress. Moreover, the structure of the chambers is very much alike; an understanding of one is almost equivalent to an understanding of the other.

Parties dominate the life of the Cortes, and it is through the party structure that the executive in turn dominates the legislature. This works despite the constitutional prohibition on party discipline—*mandato imperativo* (article 67)—that in theory makes each represenative independent, an anachronism in a political system that stresses its social or group nature. Making deputies free agents follows the tradition of liberal, individualistic nineteenth-century European democracies. In practice, the desire to progress within one's party and to have its support at election time makes the deputy accept whatever euphemism is used for discipline in the Spanish system.

Upon entering Congress, each deputy joins a parliamentary group (the equivalent of a parliamentary party in Great Britain). In order to reduce the number of groups, no group may have fewer than five members (ten in the Senate). Parliamentarians join the group that most closely approximates their political beliefs, if the group is agreeable. Naturally, each of the major parties constitutes a group unto itself. The

Cortes provides facilities like meeting rooms and secretarial help for the convenience of all groups, and all are subventioned. Assistance is distributed in part with an amount of money identical for each group and in part with an amount of money proportional to the group's size.

If a deputy is elected by a party that cannot put together the minimum number of members, that representative must either join an already existent ideologically defined group (if that is acceptable to both), or join the "mixed group," which amounts to a kind of catchall or grab bag. Any deputy who changes group affiliation during a session of parliament must join the mixed group, and may choose either to remain there or join an existing group at the next session, provided that the group accepts him or her. If there is massive defection from a group and the membership falls below the minimum, that parliamentary group ceases to exist and becomes absorbed in the mixed group. A great part of legislative activity is carried out by parliamentary groups; the legislator rarely acts as an individual (making the prohibition against party discipline even more difficult to comprehend).

Each chamber is headed by a president elected by its members. To win on the first ballot a candidate must receive an absolute majority of the votes cast; otherwise, a runoff takes place between the top two candidates, the post going to whoever receives a simple majority. In theory, the victor becomes the president of the whole chamber; in practice, he or she becomes the voice of the majority. The president regulates debate, recognizes those who have been granted prior permission to speak, and exerts discipline to keep order. The president chairs the Mesa, which operates collegially, with four vice-presidents and four secretaries in the Congress and two vice-presidents and four secretaries in the Senate. In the Congress, the four vice-presidents are chosen simultaneously, and each deputy is allowed to cast only one ballot. As a result of this voting procedure, it is almost certain that the four major parliamentary groups will be represented. The same procedure is used in the Congress to choose the four secretaries, and an almost identical system is used in the Senate. The Mesa is the directing and, in theory, the policy-making organ in each house, deciding what papers shall move among parliamentarians and in particular what the agenda of the full house and its committees will be. In practice, however, the Mesa is in charge of the bureaucratic aspects of each house; the political aspects are the purview of the Junta de Portavoces, which represents each of the parliamentary groups in each chamber. The voice of each group's representative is weighted in proportion to that group's size. The Junta is the official political voice of each chamber, to be raised if necessary against the collective voice of the Mesa when things political run counter to things bureaucratic (or vice versa) and almost inevitably against the government, particularly when the latter is composed of a single party. The Junta invariably represents many parties. The conflict between the cabinet and the Junta would, of course, be much less intense with a coalition government that reflected more or less the same fragmentation as the Junta.

The two chambers work in full house and in committees, but with few exceptions, tasks are performed in committees, particularly in permanent committees, the most important of the three Congress classifications: permanent, special, and investigatory. In the Senate, the names differ but the functions are similar. There is a permanent committee for each of the departmental ministries in the cabinet, plus several other committees with more general competency. Each parliamentary group chooses its representatives on the permanent committees in numbers proportionate to the size of the parliamentary group. Each committee chooses its chairperson from among the members, so seniority, as it exists in the U.S. Congress, for example, does not apply. The committees (which break down into subcommittees that also maintain party proportion among their members) examine and discuss all proyectos de ley (bills originating with the government) and all proposiciones de ley (bills originating with the legislature). However, governmental bills have priority under article 89, and all budget proposals and all bills relating to economic planning originate with the government (articles 134, 131). Any bill may be amended in committee, but budgetary bills, once they have been passed into law, may not be altered without the cabinet's approval.

These are the only restrictions on the power of the legislature to exert ultimate control over the government. All bills are debated by the full house as they emerge from committee. The Spanish government lacks the constitutional power of its French counterpart to call for a single up or down vote on all or part of a bill under discussion, retaining only the amendments proposed or accepted by the government. There is no constitutional division, as there is in the French constitution, between "laws," which may be regulated by the legislature, and "rules," which may be regulated by the executive. Within the general restrictions of the constitution, the legislature is competent to deal with any kind of law.

The Spanish constitution borrowed from the Italian in giving the permanent committees powers they do not have in most democracies. With the exception of constitutional amendments; treaties and other international understandings; organic and basic laws; and the budget, the chambers may delegate full legislative power to the permanent committees, obviating the necessity of having the bill debated or voted by the full house. Each house may recall that delegation at any time, however (article 75). For those who think that this process might be less than democratic, it should be remembered that in composition, the permanent committees are small-scale models of the whole chamber.

When debate does take place on the floor of the Congress or Senate, freedom to speak is severely limited. No parliamentarian may take the floor without securing prior permission from both the president of the chamber and in most cases, from the chairperson of his or her parliamentary group. Under many of the rules of each house, it is not the individual deputy who is granted permission to be heard but the parliamentary group, which then chooses a spokesperson. Once on the floor, the parliamentary member may not be interrupted, but he or she may not wander from the topic being debated nor talk beyond the allotted time. After two warnings from the president of the chamber on either of these counts, permission to speak may be revoked, making a filibuster impossible.

A bill that has passed the Congress—either by vote in the full house or, when delegated, by vote in permanent committee—moves to the Senate, where it goes through a similar procedure. Within the limit of two months, the Senate may either approve, amend, or totally reject the bill. If the bill is rejected in toto the Congress may immediately overturn the veto by ratifying the original bill by an absolute majority or, two months after the receipt of the veto, by a simple majority, the same majority it takes to accept or reject senatorial amendments. If, after two months, the Senate does nothing, a bill becomes law by default. In the Spanish constitution there is no equivalent to the U.S. conference committee, but then logic would tell us that a conference between unequals (the Senate is much less powerful than the Congress) would be politically meaningless.

What devices do the two chambers of the Cortes have to keep the government alert to their moods and opinions, considering that the party structure puts the president of the government in almost full control of the political process? The presidents of both houses are effectively agents of the majority, and although the Mesa and the Junta de Portavoces represent many parties, the majority is also dominant in those bodies due to proportional representation. The prime minister has control over the majority through his power to call for votes of confidence and to dissolve parliament. What, then, are parliament's weapons? The most powerful, of course, is censure, but this procedure is available only to the Congress, and is difficult to accomplish. Far less deadly are the rights: (1) to investigate (article 76); (2) to command the presence in the chamber of cabinet members, including the prime minister (article 110); (3) to interpellate—that is, to formally question members of the government and to debate the policies of the government and pass a motion giving the chamber's opinion, if the chamber desires to do so (article 111); (4) to initiate legislation, a right guaranteed not only to the government but also to the Congress and the Senate (article 87). Note, however, that the initiative rests with the chamber and not with the deputies or senators. Private member bills become bills of the respective chamber. This does not eliminate the pork barrel, for there is nothing to prevent a chamber from accepting all private member bills out of formality, but this is unlikely to occur, and even if it did, governmental bills always have priority. Finally, the legislature may delegate to the government lawmaking functions that normally belong to the Cortes (article 82), by decrees called *decretos legislativos* (*decretos leyes* are governmental in origin). Although the decrees represent an abdication of legislative duty in favor of the executive, the legislature itself takes the initiative to place the burden and responsibility on the government.

AUTONOMOUS REGIONS

Article 2 of the constitution declares Spain to be an indissoluable unity and then in the same sentence recognizes and guarantees the right of the nationalities and regions that make up the nation to proclaim their autonomy—without mentioning what this seemingly anomalous hybrid would be called. This omission was not an oversight, for definition is dangerous where certain words—federalism or separatism, for example—may trigger an explosive reaction. The reticence toward clarity has roots deep in Spain's past, for the forces of centralism and regionalism have fought bloody battles for centuries. The brief history of Spain sketched in the early chapters of this book was written in part to catalog this contest and to lay the background for understanding the struggle that still goes on today. Except for the Basque extremists, fortunately, the struggle is now taking place within a peaceful and constitutionally established arena.

The unity that Rome brought to Spain and that, after the fall of Rome, the Visigoths reestablished under a single monarch ended with the Islamic invasion. The reestablishment of that harmonious unity has in many ways been the goal of all subsequent Spanish history. Since the Reconquest, there have been recurrent periods of unity, but these cycles have been achieved most often by the suppression of local rights. Recall that Muslim Spain was a single entity only during the brief reign of Abd ar-Rahman III. Before his reign, various Muslim kingdoms on the peninsula had defied Al-Andalus, and seventy years after his death, the caliphate had once again shattered into independent, warring taifas. Christian Spain was not unified until the reign of Ferdinand and Isabella, and even then, the two monarchs maintained their separate kingdoms even after their marriage created Spain by bringing the kingdoms together. The Catholic Kings did not destroy the fueros that had been so doggedly obtained from their ancestors. Their Hapsburg descendants ruled a unified nation-state but recognized the rights of the fueros, bowing to political reality. It was the Bourbons, emulating their French relatives, who brought modern unity to Spain by tearing down most of the regional fueros (those of Catalonia, Valencia, Aragon and the Balearic Islands) and emasculating those that they left standing (in Navarre and the Basque provinces). The history of the Bourbons is rife with conflict between Madrid and the regions that would not stay suppressed. The First Republic was committed to federalism, but it lasted only a year (1873-1874), and its constitution never came into force. The restored Bourbons tightened the centralization of the country. The Second Republic (1931–1936) recognized the validity of regionalism and had begun decentralization when the Civil War broke out, partly over this very issue. The victorious Franco—even though he himself was a native of one of the regions demanding recognition, Galicia—crushed all resistance to his rule from Madrid, even forbidding people to speak their regional tongues in the privacy of their homes.

The constitution of 1978 recognizes the centrifugal forces of the nation (the regions attempting to pull away from Madrid), but it also recognizes the centripetal forces of the state (Madrid attempting to pull the regions under the hegemony of a single sovereignty). Both forces have a history too long for their validity to be denied. The unity of Spain is as much a heritage as racial and regional separateness. The constitution does not predetermine what the new Spain will be like when the regions seeking autonomy make their claims. Article 143 makes autonomy voluntary, although all the provinces of Spain have now been carved into regions. There are few restrictions limiting autonomy. Each province that seeks to join with others to form a region must have a contiguous border with at least one of the other provinces. Article 145 prohibits the federation of regions. Article 143 stipulates that regions are to be formed by several provinces with historical, cultural, or economic backgrounds in common, but article 144 provides for a region made from a single province (the area of Madrid, for example) where the pre-conditions of article 143 cannot be met.

Two ways were established to achieve autonomy: fast (article 151) and slow (article 143). The slow pace seems favored by the constitution, but the rapid path is made available for those impatient provinces whose identity has long been recognized (like Catalonia and the Basque country) and whose people are overwhelmingly committed to autonomy. Most of the areas of Spain do not have this kind of identity, and the slow pace was preferred for those provinces that would need time to create a viable region. For the slow track, the initiative to begin the process must be approved by the legislatures of the interested provinces and by two-thirds of the voters in those municipalities whose population represents a majority of the electoral census of the province (the capital cities). The requirements must be fulfilled within six months, and if the initiative fails it may not be attempted again for five years.

The quick route to autonomy is more difficult; it requires a massive commitment by the provinces that seek to use it. As with the slow pace, the initiative rests with the provincial legislatures, but the percentage of voters necessary to begin the process is raised to three-quarters in the municipalities whose population represents at least a majority of each province's electoral census. After these requirements have been met, the initiative is submitted to referendum in the provinces involved and must be accepted by an absolute majority of the electors of each province.

If the initiative (fast or slow) is successful, a statute is formulated by the legislatures of the provinces involved plus the deputies and senators representing the provinces in the national Cortes. The statute is then submitted to the Cortes for enactment into law, and with the king's signature, an autonomous region is born. A final caution should be mentioned. There is no provision in the constitution that determines what would happen if one or both of the chambers of the Cortes refuse to ratify the statute.

The section of the constitution entitled "Concerning the Autonomous Communities" clearly demonstrates the tension that pervaded the constituent assembly. The call for a strong central government was imperative, but the demand for regional self-determination was equally exigent. A balance had to be found without alienating either the centralists or the regionalists; terminology had to be carefully chosen and specificity sacrificed if the document was to be ratified. Federalism, for example, was a taboo word, and the details of how the national government would exert its supremacy over the autonomous regions were never spelled out.

The constitution allows the creation of autonomous communities with executive, legislative, and judicial powers, providing for true regional government and not merely the administrative decentralization of the national executive function. Article 152 stipulates that each autonomous community will have a unicameral legislative assembly with deputies elected for a four-year term by universal suffrage using a system of proportional representation that guarantees a voice to the various parts of the region. The assembly nominates from among its members the president (or prime minister), who is in turn appointed by the king. The Council of Government (or cabinet) is also chosen from among the members of the assembly following a procedure to be determined by each assembly. Even though political parties are not mentioned, it seems logical to assume that party politics would dominate all elections within the regional legislature. Together the president and the council constitute the executive, which is politically responsible to the assembly, and can be removed by it. Like the Cortes, the regional legislature may operate either as a whole house or in committee, and in addition to its principal function of lawmaking for the region, it also may initiate law before the Cortes (article 87). Furthermore, the assembly elects the senators who represent the autonomous community in the national Senate (article 69).

Article 152 of the constitution allows each autonomous community to create a high court of justice to resolve judicial conflict within the borders of the region without in any way prejudicing the nationwide authority of the Supreme Court in Madrid. It should be pointed out for the sake of accuracy that article 152 applies only to those regions that take the fast route to autonomy (article 151), but logic tells us that the provisions will be extended to those that take the slow route (article 143).

Article 149 lists the areas that are the exclusive responsibility of the central government: nationality and immigration; international relations; defense and the armed forces; customs and tariffs; the monetary system; general, overall national planning; and the calling of national referenda. Article 148 lists the powers and responsibilities that belong to the autonomous regions, which include the regulation of municipal boundaries; urbanization and housing; highways, railways, and public works within their borders; private airports and marinas (recreational facilities only); irrigation, canals, and flood control within their regions; and a wide spectrum of touristic and cultural activities including the right to teach native languages.

Article 149 also lists the powers that belong exclusively to the central government but that may be delegated to the autonomous regions. These deal primarily with regional transportation and traffic control—air, sea, rail, and road; telegraph and radio communications; the post office; meteorological service; cultural activities such as the restoration and preservation of national monuments; and the regulation of academic and professional titles.

This division of power would be recognized by any student of government and politics as a federal system irrespective of what the Spaniards choose to call it, yet Jorge de Esteban and Luis López Guerra make the case that the Spanish system is not classically federal, thus avoiding the use of the inflammatory term. They contend that in a federal system the component units enjoy full power from the moment the political system comes into existence, whereas in the Spanish system article 148 of the constitution says: "The

autonomous communities may assume competence in the
following areas. . . ." The Spanish regions may or may not
choose to assume the full panoply of power constitutionally
available to them. It would seem, however, that the Spanish
commentators' reasoning will fail once all the communities
assumed full authority. Moreover, it is almost certain that all
the regions would immediately choose to be fully armed with
the powers provided by the constitution. Those that defer
their decisions could be at a serious disadvantage when dealing
with fully empowered communities.

Perhaps the provisions most likely to produce conflict
between the central government and the autonomous regions
reside in article 150, which allows the Cortes to permit one
or all of the regional assemblies to make laws in areas normally
reserved to the national legislature. The Cortes may also
transfer, to one or all of the regional cabinet and bureaucracy,
functions that normally belong to the national executive. In
addition, and most potentially troublesome of all, article 150
permits the national government to pass laws that regularize
the authoritative decisions of the autonomous communities,
even in those areas reserved to the latter's competence, if the
national common good demands it. Obviously, the potential
for conflict between the national and regional governments
is enormous; the "common good" can be a highly contentious
term.

To protect the regions from the possible encroachment
of the central government, article 150 requires that the national
government obtain an absolute majority vote in each chamber
of the Cortes before it may act to regularize the behavior of
the autonomous regions. In order to protect the central government from the improper behavior of an autonomous
community, the article stipulates that the laws passed at the
regional level under the delegated power of the national
government will be subject to scrutiny by the Cortes. Of
course, any law passed at any level is subject to the challenge
of constitutionality heard in the Constitutional Court. An
administrative or executive function transferred to a regional
government under article 150 will be monitored by the national
prime minister and the cabinet, with the higher executive

level overseeing the lower. Administrative oversight in general will fall to the government's delegate provided for in article 154 of the constitution. The delegate, appointed by the government, is the liaison between the central government and the autonomous region and directs the bureaucratic functions of the national government in the autonomous region; where necessary the delegate coordinates the administrative functions of the two entities.

Finally, under article 155 the national government has a reserve of control to be used in extraordinary circumstances. If an autonomous community does not conform to the obligations of the constitution or acts in a way that gravely threatens the national interest, the national government may take "the necessary steps" to compel the region to fulfill its obligations or to alter its behavior. Before it acts, however, the national government must first warn the president of the autonomous community. If the warning is ignored, the government may then take action once it has received the approval of the absolute majority of the Senate, the chamber that represents the autonomous communities in the Cortes.

The financial viability of the autonomous regions is guaranteed in articles 156, 157, and 158 of the constitution. The regions may levy taxes; they may be reimbursed with part or all of certain national taxes; they may be awarded funds from the national government so that essential public services are properly carried out throughout the entire country; and they may receive monies out of the Interterritorial Compensation Fund, a kind of equalization grant designed to compensate the poorer regions.

9
Political Parties

    The UCD no longer exists. It disintegrated following the elections of October 1982, which enabled the PSOE to form the government with an absolute majority and gave the opposition to the AP. How this occurred and what the consequences might be for Spanish politics will be discussed in Chapter 10, but for readers to understand the role of the UCD they should know now about the collapse of the party even before we discuss its birth. It is difficult to accept that a party indispensable for almost six years should now be dead.

DISCONTINUITY IN THE SPANISH PARTY SYSTEM

Perhaps the demise of the short-lived UCD indicates the tenuous nature of the Spanish party system, which has yet to stabilize. The major characteristic of the system is its youth; for all practical purposes, Spanish political parties came into being after January 1977. Even the Socialist party created in 1879 and the Communist party, which dates to 1921, developed new forms. The Spanish parties are unlike those of the established European democracies, whose parties evolved and matured over long, relatively uninterrupted periods. Nor do they resemble those of former dictatorships that established democratic systems after World War II.

The twentieth-century development of Spanish parties (most of them corrupted by the political system in which they operated during the last decades of the nineteenth and the early decades of the twentieth centuries) was interrupted by the dictatorship of Primo de Rivera from 1923 to 1929. Continuity was shakily restablished during the brief and chaotic Second Republic (1931–1936), and then finally broken completely after 1939, when the Civil War ended. In reality, parties had already been destroyed in those parts of Spain that had fallen under Franco's control as the fighting progressed. On September 13, 1936, two months after the outbreak of hostilities, the Junta de Defensa Nacional, then the governing body of Nationalist Spain, outlawed all political parties. The ban stayed in force, except for the official FET y de las JONS (later renamed the National Movement), until February 1977. Note the absence of the detested word "party." For Franco, political parties were the scourge of Spain and the cause (not the result) of Spanish divisiveness. Franco's attack on parties during the war and his relentless pursuit of their remnants after the war was over effectively ended party activity for 36 or 39 years, depending on whether one dates from 1939 or 1936.

When parties were legalized in 1977 there was almost no one who could link the present to the past. By contrast to Franco, who ruled for almost 40 years, Hitler ruled for 12 years (from 1933 to 1945) and Mussolini, 21 (1922–1943). When parties were resuscitated in Germany and Italy after World War II there were politicians ready to begin again who had been active before the dictatorships: Konrad Adenauer and Alcide di Gasperi, to name only two. In Spain, there were but a very few; one was Santiago Carrillo, the Communist leader. Carrillo's forty years of exile had put him out of touch with the reality within Spain, however, and after his triumphant return home in December 1976, his accomplishments as party leader (in contrast to his personal contribution in easing the transition to democracy) can only be called a failure. Dolores Ibárurri, the legendary la Pasionaria of the Civil War, also returned, but she was in her eighties, and her years of exile in the Soviet Union made her value to the emerging Spanish democracy little more than symbolic. The authors of the Foessa report had the following comments on the discontinuity of Spanish parties:

The relative discontinuity has positive aspects. The present-day parties are less affected by the myths of the past, that is, by the problems and failures that preceded the Civil War. But there are also some negative aspects: the absence of the historic memory of past errors and above all the lack of democratic, parliamentary experience of the new political class.[1]

Finally, a few words should be said about the attitude of the average Spaniard toward political parties. In 1975, when asked by pollsters about their liberties, the Spaniards placed the need for parties fifth on the list of essential political possessions. First was freedom of the press; then freedom of religion; third was freedom to create labor unions; and fourth, freedom to create private universities. Much of this attitude has been attributed to the four decades of propaganda poured out by Franco on the evils of parties. This prejudice, the result of socialization deeply planted and difficult to root out, continues even today, and many in Spain who think seriously about politics feel that this mentality obstructs the development of faith in democracy. Many Spaniards misunderstand just what politics and political parties can and cannot accomplish in a free society.

PARTIES OF THE TRANSITION

Unión del Centro Democrático (UCD)

The UCD, or Democratic Center Union, was the great party of the transition. Ahead of its time, a fortuitous creation that enabled Spain to survive Franco, the UCD died because it was essentially artificial, alien to the present Spanish political soil. It was a kind of catchall party in an emergent democracy whose societal elements had not yet found a common denominator (or denominators) for the long haul of democracy. In the short run, the UCD was an incarnation of the hope that temporarily eclipsed a heterogeneity too vast to be accommodated by a single political party. Once the hope (the creation of a democratic Spain) became a reality, the day-today political will necessary to make the creation thrive proved too taxing for the elements that made up the UCD.

The UCD began as a federation called the Unión del Centro (Center Union), composed of fifteen parties that reflected mostly Christian Democratic, Social Democratic, or Liberal (European usage) philosophies. The threads that held them together were their rejection of Francoism and their commitment to political change, but the nature of the change and the shape that the new political system would take lay hidden by ideological differences. It is unlikely that this motley association would have had the great political force it came to possess if Adolfo Suárez had not announced in early May 1977 that he would be a candidate for Congress in the June 1977 elections and would join the Center Union as an independent, unaffiliated with any of the constituent parties. Until his announcement, Suárez had had no political identification; he was prime minister in a personal, not a party, capacity, appointed by and loyal only to the king. After his embrace of the party, the Center Union changed its name to UCD and changed its position from anti-Franco to prosystem. The system was represented by the king, Suárez, and by the governmental associates the prime minister brought along with him into the party. The new UCD became the party in power, the party of the incumbents, who have the advantage in any political system. Suárez was able to turn the resources of the state to the advantage of his and his party's electoral campaign. Moreover, in a country where deference to those in power had been instilled for decades, this fusion of political power and democratic commitment gave the UCD enormous political strength. The way the resources of the state were placed behind the UCD would scandalize a good British or U.S. citizen. The UCD's use of the state bureaucracy and the favoritism shown to the UCD by radio and television, all of which are owned and operated by the state, came under heavy criticism from the opposition, which could do little about what it considered to be abuse. In defense of such cavalier behavior on the part of those in control of the government perhaps one could say that at least things were done for a good cause: the delivery of democracy to Spain.

Moreover, at that moment in Spanish political evolution, the rules of the game of democratic behavior (i.e., democratic action as opposed to democratic words) were in their earliest formative stage.

The UCD became even more the party of those in power when it won the largest number of votes in the 1977 elections and the largest number of seats in the Congress. It won only a plurality, not an absolute majority, however, and formed a minority government. The party was able to stay in power because of support from the smaller regional parties in the legislature. Suárez then moved to consolidate the party behind him and on June 23, a week following the elections, announced that the coalition of parties that made up the UCD would merge to form a single entity. The formal creation of the new UCD took place on August 5, 1977, and the party held its first congress the following October. By his action, Suárez effectively cut the ties between the leaders of the formerly separate parties and their now disbanded organizations, creating what the media called the "barons," who spoke for various political viewpoints but who were deprived of an institutionalized base outside the UCD. They became totally dependent upon Suárez, who alone controlled the access to power.

The new consolidated party was essentially a pragmatic, centrist organization whose primary goal was the winning and keeping of power. Because of its diverse background, however, its philosophy was somewhat amorphous and freeform, designed to attract as many voters as possible. Luis García San Miguel described the party in two different ways:

> The UCD presented itself as the resultant of a kind of triple synthesis: *between* forces emerging out of Francoism and forces emerging out of the opposition; *between* ideals and aspirations from the right and others from the left; finally *among* Christian Democratic, Social Democratic, and Liberal ideologies.[2]

> As Gasperi said of the Christian Democracy [in Italy], the UCD was a party of the center, playing the politics of the left with votes of the right.[3]

The party believed in a state that was strong and positive but meanwhile protected civil and human rights; it believed in the unity of Spain but supported regionalist claims. The UCD stood for the separation of church and state but recognized the special place of Catholicism in Spanish society. Its foreign policy sought the integration of Spain into a democratic Europe while maintaining close ties with the United States. As García San Miguel said, if we equate the Right with capitalism and the Left with socialism, then "we would have to say that the program of the UCD is clearly rightist, much like the program of other Liberal and Christian Democratic parties in the West."[4] If the Right is proreligion and the Left is antireligion, then again the UCD would have to be considered rightist. Still, Suárez took a tolerant stand on the legalization of divorce and the decriminalization of adultery, positions similar to those of the Left, and it was he who legalized the Communist party, called for the first free elections in forty-one years, and supported amnesty for terrorists.

Obviously, the party suffered from internal tension from the very beginning, and that stress eventually pulled the party apart once the initial transition to democracy seemed to be sufficiently accomplished for the efferent forces within the party to begin the struggle to restructure it in their own images. For the Social Democrats, the party was too rightist: too slow to reform society; too willing to allow the Francoist infrastructure (the bureaucracy, the police, the armed forces, the university system, the world of banking and finance) to stay in place; too committed to unalloyed capitalism.

For the Christian Democrats, the party was too leftist: too willing to secularize; too tolerant of permissive behavior like divorce, adultery, and abortion; too ready to pact with the Left, the policy of consensus. The details of how these forces finally destroyed the UCD will be discussed in Chapter 10.

Partido Socialista de Obrero Español (PSOE)

The Spanish Socialist Worker's party is the oldest party in Spain, but the discontinuity spoken about earlier robbed it of most of its ties to the past. The PSOE was effectively reborn in October 1974, at the congress held in Surenes near Paris. Control of the party went to a group of young men and women of the post–Civil War generation whose ideology was Marxist and revolutionary. The "young turks," of whom the most prominent was Felipe González, did not live in exile but had identified with what remained of the exiled party as the living embodiment of classic Spanish socialism. They were a part of the majority sector of the party called *renovado* (renewed); the minority sector of the party, called *histórico* (historic) was for the most part made up of older, more moderate Socialists with Social Democratic leanings. Both persuasions sought to use the magic initials PSOE. In fact, when the party was legalized in Spain in February 1977, it was the históricos who were the first to register their application with the government, and for a short time they carried the official Socialist label. The anomaly was soon corrected, however, and the government recognized the majority renovados as the legitimate heirs to the party's name and mystique.

This was not the only party speaking for socialism, however. During the Franco regime men of great stature within Spain, particularly in the universities and in journalism, had begun to oppose his rule. Their careful opposition was usually within the limits of what the regime would tolerate, but these activists were present in Spain and not living out of harm's way in exile. They were equally vulnerable to suppression by the regime and to attack from the party in exile, which accused them of opportunism. Among the Socialists in Spain was the eminent professor Enrique Tierno Galván, whose attacks on the regime became so intense that in 1965 Franco had him removed for life from his university chair. When political parties were legalized in 1977, Tierno and his followers felt that they had earned their places in the political system that Suárez and the king were creating, and they rejected the claim of the PSOE that it alone was the voice of socialism in Spain. Tierno organized a socialist alternative to PSOE called the Partido Socialista Popular (PSP, Popular Socialist Party), which presented its own lists of candidates in the elections of June 1977.

It was the PSOE and not the PSP that galvanized the nonCommunist Left, and the PSOE declared its principles at the first congress held on Spanish soil in over forty-one years. Attending as guests were most of the great names in European Socialism: Pietro Nenni (Italy), François Mitterrand (France), Willy Brandt (West Germany), Olof Palme (Sweden), and Michael Foote (Great Britain). Suárez allowed the congress to convene in Madrid in October 1976, two months before the party became legal. The PSOE claimed that it was "a class party, and as a consequence a Marxist and democratic party of the masses."

> We are a class party because we defend and fight for the historic project of the working class: the disappearance of the exploitation of man by man and the construction of a classless society. . . . We are Marxist in that we believe in the scientific method . . . and that class conflict . . . is the motor of society. . . . We define ourselves as democratic because we are in agreement that the internal organization of the party should be scrupulously democratic. . . . The PSOE defines itself as socialist because its program and behavior lead to the takeover of the means of capitalist production through the assumption of political and economic power by the working class and the socializing of the means of production, distribution, and monetary exchange. We understand socialism to be both a goal and a process that leads to that goal, and our beliefs compel us to reject any accommodation with or simple reform of capitalism.[5]

The PSOE entered the 1977 elections with the above ideology, yet during the campaign a great effort was made to soften the party's image before the electorate in order to win votes, as evidenced by the following passage from an *El Pais* article:

> A short time ago a socialist wrote in *El Pais* a lucid and interesting article in which he explained that the characteristic elements of the PSOE defined and approved of at the last

congress were: Marxism, republicanism, class warfare, and revolution. And he went on to say that none of these words had appeared in the electoral propaganda nor had any of them been spoken by the highest authority of the party [Felipe González] in his talks on television.[6]

If moderation had already begun before the elections, its outcome may have prompted González to become even more accommodating, more flexible, and more pragmatic if he entertained hopes of his party someday forming a government with himself as prime minister. A working-class nation had given the plurality of its support neither to the Communists nor to the Socialists but to a center-right coalition whose vocabulary was comfortingly temperate.

In October 1977, González negotiated with Prime Minister Suárez and the other major political leaders in parliament to create the Moncloa Pacts, whose articles accepted a reformed, capitalist, free market economy at odds with socialist doctrine. In late May 1978, when the Socialists and the centrists arrived at an impasse in their negotiations on the draft of the constitution, Suárez and González instructed their seconds-in-command to work out a compromise—the crucial Suárez-González agreement—thereby insuring the successful passage of the draft through the Cortes. Earlier in the year, González had begun to mend the rift between the PSP, which had performed poorly in the 1977 elections, and the PSOE. In April 1978 the PSOE absorbed the PSP, making Tierno Galván honorary president of the PSOE. A few days later, González broached the topic that clearly revealed his commitment to moderation and to the movement of his party away from ideological militancy. He proposed that at the next congress of the PSOE to be held in May 1979, the adjective "Marxist" be dropped from the party's definition. In the meantime, the party went once again to the polls on March 1, 1979, in the general elections called by Suárez following the nation's acceptance of the constitution in the referendum held in December 1978. The ideology presented by the PSOE to the electorate during the campaign was the same as that presented in the election of June 1977, and the response of the people was almost identical: The UCD won 35.5 percent of the votes and 167 seats in the Congress (34.8 percent and 165 seats in 1977); the PSOE won 30.8 percent of the vote and 121 seats in the Congress (29.4 percent and 118 seats in 1977). The Socialists met in convention in May 1979 to face the reality that after two elections (1977 and 1979) and two referenda (1976 and 1978) they still were the second party in Spain. The Marxists at the congress were convinced that the reason for the failure lay in González's conciliatory behavior, which compromised the ideology of the party to accommodate what they considered to be a capitalist, bourgeois political system. They believed the remedy was to restate and live with conviction the party platform set forth in 1976. For those who defended González, the remedy lay in stripping the PSOE of outworn theories no longer suitable for Spain, i.e., Marxism. The Spanish people were obviously wary of the Socialists despite the charisma of Felipe González, and even his own moderation had evidently been insufficient to convince a large enough majority (or even plurality) that the Socialists were democratically trustworthy as long as the party maintained its revolutionary stance. The Marxists won the day at the congress, but in a carefully calculated and eminently theatrical gesture, González resigned his position as secretary-general (the effective but not titular head of the party). The calculated performance was risky because a new leader could have been selected to replace him. But González was a pragmatic, ambitious politician eager to lead Spain, and he realized that there was no one in the party who even approached his stature and popularity. The foreseeable future of the party seemed bleak without Felipe— who is known in Spain as just "Felipe": The last name is superfluous, which should give the reader some idea of his celebrity. The gamble paid off. In the extraordinary congress called in September 1979, González was reelected secretary-general, and the term "Marxism" was beautifully finessed, satisfying both Marxists and non-Marxists.

The PSOE considers Marxism to be a critical, theoretical, undogmatic instrument for the analysis and transformation of society gathering together the various Marxist and non-Marxist contributions that have come together to make socialism the great liberalizing alternative of our people's time, completely respectful of people's individual beliefs.[7]

The Partido Comunista Español (PCE)

The Spanish Communist party has perhaps received more credit than it should for its role in the transition. The PCE's poor showing in the elections of 1977 and 1979 indicates that the party was not a potent force among the electorate, and the 1982 elections almost eliminated it completely from national politics, at least for the time being. But the mystique of the party and the bravura of its leader, Santiago Carrillo, made its voice one of the most carefully heeded in the early period of the transition before the elections of 1977 showed that the PCE's approval or disapproval of political change had not been that important. Students of Spanish history and politics should not find this surprising, however. The party has never played a significant role in Spanish politics. Its part in the Second Republic was minor. It elected no deputies to the 484-member Cortes in 1931, 1 in 1934, and 17 in 1936. It was only after the intervention of the Soviet Union in the Civil War at the request of the desperate republic (which sought but received no aid from the United States, France, or Great Britain) that Communist influence increased enormously in Spain—the price the republic paid for Soviet help. Because Franco proclaimed that he was fighting to save Spain and the world from communism, and because the Communists willingly accepted the mantle of the thwarted savior of the Spanish democracy—defeated by the intervention of the Axis powers and by the neglect of the Western democracies—their aura grew in Spain and throughout much of the world, nourished by the exiles who fled Spain after Franco's victory in 1939. To their credit, the Communists organized the most effective underground opposition to Franco in the early years of his regime, and in later years it was once again the Communists who organized the covert Workers' Commissions that infiltrated the official trade union, the syndicates, that structured and controlled labor. These efforts did not legitimize the Communists electorally in post-Franco Spain, however. The Spanish Communists (and most political observers as well) had expected that their courageous clandestine activity in Spain during the Franco years and their posture as heirs to the republic would accomplish for them what activity in the underground had accomplished for the French and Italian Communists, who had been generously rewarded at the polls after World War II for their commitment to these nations and for their heroism.

If the party itself was less then successful, its leader, Santiago Carrillo, was undeniably a powerful presence in post-Franco Spain, and his moderation contributed significantly to Spain's relatively smooth transition to democracy, in particular his acceptance of the monarchy and of the highly symbolic new Spanish flag and his role in the creation of the constitution. Coming home after almost four decades of exile, Carrillo made a dramatic first public appearance in Madrid in December 1976. His arrest on December 22 and unexpected release on December 30 symbolized the joyful yet painful return of all of the men and women who had ever been hounded by Franco. Carrillo was free and he was a hero. As already described, the cry from those who supported freedom for his party became the cry for freedom for all political persuasions, no matter how heretical.

Even before his return to Spain, however, Carrillo had already begun to temper his ideology, whether out of true commitment to liberalization or out of opportunism in his quest for political power, no one can be sure. In July 1976, Carrillo spoke in what later would be labeled Eurocommunist terminology, separating himself from Moscow's domination:

> Yes . . . we had our pope, our Vatican and we thought we were predestined to triumph. But as we mature and become less of a church, we must become more national, closer to reality. We must see that each individual has his private life, his individual sense of things. I told the last party executive meeting that a person's preference of friends, of music and literature, whether to be religious or atheist, has nothing to

do with the party. The party can only be concerned with problems of politics and social struggle. . . .

And why not make a comparison with Luther. . . . Nowadays, he wouldn't be burned by the Inquisition. Heretics usually turn out to be all right. They are ahead of their time, but after all they are right. We want communists to be heretics. When we are conservatives we are no longer right. . . .

We want a type of socialism with universal suffrage, alternation of government, not control of power for the communists but an alliance of forces that in no way would allow a communist monopoly. . . . We mean the Communist party could be in one coalition government and if it lost out in the next elections it would be outside.[8]

These were the words of Carrillo speaking personally before his return to Spain in December 1976. Following the legalization of the PCE in April 1977, the Spanish party made no modification in its statutes to reflect Carrillo's new philosophy. The PCE went into the 1977 elections with its Marxist-Leninist ideology intact, winning only 9.3 percent of the vote and twenty seats in the Congress. In a reaction similar to that later taken by Felipe González, Carrillo moved to demonstrate to the electorate that he and his party were worthy of trust. Carrillo took part in the negotiations that led to the Moncloa Pacts in October 1977, many of whose articles were contrary to communist economic theory. In April 1978, while the draft of the constitution was being hammered out, Carrillo officiated at the historic Ninth Congress of the PCE, which eliminated the word "Leninist" from the party's self-definition, maintaining that "today it is no longer fitting to consider Leninism to be the Marxism of our time."[9] The delegates also excised the concept of the dictatorship of the proletariat and embraced Carrillo's Eurocommunist philosophy. The party was then redefined as Marxist, revolutionary, and democratic.

The PCE presented itself to the electorate in the elections of March 1, 1979, under its new Eurocommunist banner, but the response from the people was little different from that in 1977. The PCE won 10.9 percent of the vote and 23 seats in Congress, compared to 9.3 percent and 20 seats in 1977.

The new face of the party had not convinced the Spanish people that its heart and mind had changed as well. A great part of the popular skepticism could be attributed to the internecine war that had begun to rage within the party itself. Three factions contended for the leadership, which did not shift, however, until after the party's debacle in the national elections of October 1982. One faction was pro-Soviet and attributed the party's plight to the adulteration of its classic doctrines. Why should the people vote for a Eurocommunist program when there was already an almost identical one offered by the PSOE? A return to basics would swing the national leftist vote back to the Communists. A second faction was pro-Eurocommunist but against Carrillo, who, it claimed, ran the party internally like an autocrat, allowing no dissent and purging those who dared challenge him. Like the pro-Soviets, this group wanted to oust Carrillo, but whereas the former believed Carrillo had corrupted the party, the latter believed that he had deceived it, showing one face to the public and another to the party's militants. This group wanted the democracy exhibited externally to be practiced internally, and it attributed the party's electoral weakness to its internal contradictions. The third faction was made up of those loyal to Carrillo.

Alianza Popular (AP)

The Popular Alliance is synonymous with Manuel Fraga Iribarne, perhaps the most complex personality in contemporary Spanish politics. Fraga was considered a liberal when he served Franco as minister of information and tourism from 1962 to 1969, and his name became a household word when he engineered the first opening up of the regime with the Press Law of 1966. He was purged from the ministry in 1969 by Franco, who insinuated that his policies to liberalize the media, including entertainment, and to attract tourists had begun to corrupt public taste and morals. Fraga was only a liberal when compared to the conservatives who made up much of the Franco establishment. After the caudillo's death, Fraga's natural conservatism came forth amidst the liberalizing

elite that was moving into predominance after the resignation
of Prime Minister Arias Navarro. Many agree with distinguished British historian Raymond Carr and coauthor Juan
Pablo Fusi that Fraga's hardening political stance became
more pronounced after his experience as minister of the
interior (in charge of the police and internal security) in the
Arias government, when he was forced to deal with the
violence that continued to sweep Spain.[10] Perhaps it was then
that Fraga's strategy for the transition took shape, a strategy
rejected when Juan Carlos chose Suárez to head the government that replaced Arias.

Fraga's plan for political change would have maintained
the positive things that had come out of Francoism. After
all, the unprecedented national prosperity of the 1970s had
come about as a result of decisions made by the generalissimo
in the early 1950s. The Civil War and Franco were realities
that had to be accepted—without any wish to recapture the
past, however, as the extreme right proclaimed it wanted to
do. Fraga intended to modify the Francoist system slowly,
keeping intact its basic structure, including probably even the
syndicates. This strategy differed from that of Suárez, who
was using the existing Francoist laws and institutions to
restructure the system totally, abiding by the letter of those
laws but not by their spirit. Finally, Fraga would have closed
the system permanently to certain parties and groups: the
Communists, above all, but also those who sought to weaken
the unity of the state, such as the regional extremists.

Fraga's program became the basis for his own political
group, Reforma Democrática (Democractic Reform), which in
October 1976 federated with six other rightist groups to form
Alianza Popular, which celebrated its first congress in March
1977, two months before the June elections. The AP platform
was right wing, formulated by leaders who, with one exception,
had all served at one time or another as ministers in Franco's
cabinets. They took pride in their identification with the
former regime, while maintaining that they sought no nostalgic
revival and intended to play by the democratic rules of the
game. This was interpreted to mean that if the AP were to
win the elections it would not use its power to reconstruct

Francoism. However, the party's reassurance failed to convince the electorate, which gave the AP only 8.4 percent of the vote and 16 seats in the Congress in the 1977 elections.

The two sources that the party had counted on for support turned out to be far weaker than expected: the residual appeal of Franco, which party members felt was still very strong among the people; and the vote of the many functionaries to whom Franco had given employment—a veritable army of doorkeepers, building superintendents, janitors, porters, cleaning women, lottery ticket salespeople (reserved for the handicapped), who were barely employable even in the early years of Francoism. If democracy put an end to featherbedding, much of this army would face unemployment.

The Popular Alliance held together while the constitution was being created, and Fraga's was the dominant voice from the Right on the Committee on Constitutional Affairs. At times he raised it viciously against those articles in the drafts of the document that he considered to be "red." Yet after the constitution was approved by the Cortes, Fraga urged AP supporters to follow his example and vote their approval in the December referendum. The reasons for this about-face (called duplicity by the party's right wing) are not fully known, but Fraga probably realized that his future in the political system, which the constitution was about to usher in, would be spent permanently in the backwater of the extreme right if he did not approve the document and move toward the center.

Fraga's action provoked the departure of two of the AP's most conservative members: Gonzalo Fernández de la Mora, whose ideology was very close to the extreme right (and thus close to opposing the democratic system) and Federico Silva Muñoz. This withdrawal automatically made the AP more moderate, a posture already endorsed by the younger members who spoke for a tempered and civilized right at the party's second congress, held in January 1978. Fraga's sympathy with this more moderate, centrist position can be seen in the following remarks:

Obviously the center is one thing, and the UCD of Suárez is something else. The center includes many people, and the UCD is only a small bureaucratic machine that Suárez has set up and manipulates for his own convenience. . . . With respect to the right, we are not going to speak about the right but about the center-right which is what we are and have always said we have been.[11]

In the elections of 1979, the centrist electorate stayed loyal to the UCD. The AP fared even more poorly then it had in 1977, dropping to 5.8 percent of the vote (8.4 in 1977) and 9 seats in the Congress (16 in 1977). The AP seemed to be in an irreversible decline, yet in the elections of 1982 the UCD was obliterated. The PSOE won the plurality of votes and the absolute majority of seats in the Cortes, and the AP that had appeared moribund three years earlier emerged the second largest party in Spain.

NOTES

1. *Informe sociológico sobre el cambio político en España, 1975–1981* (Madrid: Editorial Euramérica, S.A., 1981), p. 343.

2. Luis García San Miguel, "Las ideologias políticas en la España actual," *Sistema* 40 (January 1981):64.

3. Luis García San Miguel, *Teoría de la transición* (Madrid: Editora Nacional, 1981), p. 141.

4. Ibid., p. 118.

5. Resoluciones del Congreso del PSOE de 1976, Madrid, 1977 (folleto del Partido).

6. *El Pais*, September 18, 1977.

7. Antonio Bar, "El sistema de partidos en España: Ensayo de caracterización," *Sistema* 47 (March 1982):24.

8. *New York Times*, July 7, 1976.

9. *Cambio 16*, April 2, 1978.

10. Raymond Carr and Juan Pablo Fusi, *Spain: Dictatorship to Democracy*, 2d ed. (London: George Allen and Unwin, 1981), pp. 212–213.

11. *Cambio 16*, February 26, 1978.

Part 3
Political Crises

10

Collapse of the Center

The Spaniards went to the polls for the first time under the new constitution on March 1, 1979, the fourth electoral venture since Franco's death in 1975. The first three were the referendum of 1976, the 1977 elections, and the referendum of 1978. Turnout was poor, perhaps due to weariness from having just voted three months previously; or perhaps this was a premature manifestation of the cynicism that seeps into any working democracy. Perhaps the abstention rate was an indication that Spanish democracy was becoming healthier; citizens apparently felt that they could ignore their newly acquired electoral duty with impunity. Whatever the explanation, political participation had been falling steadily since the first balloting in 1976 and 1977, when the abstention rate was 22.6 percent and 21.6 percent respectively. In 1978 and 1979, the abstention rate was 32.3 percent and 33.6 percent. In 1979, the electorate had been expanded by almost 3.5 million by lowering the voting age to 18, but the number of votes cast dropped by almost 317,000.

The basic power structure at the national level remained more or less the same as a result of the elections, however. The UCD picked up 2 seats in the 350-seat Congress, once again giving it the plurality with 167 (165 in 1977); the PSOE won 121 seats (118 in 1977); the PCE, 23 (20 in 1977); and the AP (under a temporary new name, Democratic Coalition) received 9, down from 16 in 1977. Juan Carlos once again nominated Adolfo Suárez to be prime minister, and Suárez was confirmed on March 30, 1979. But if the power structure remained about the same, there was evidence that political change was in the making. For the first time, extremist parties won seats in the Cortes. Herri Batasuna (HB, United People), the political counterpart of the most violent Basque terrorist group, ETA militar, won 3 seats in the Congress (to show contempt for the political system, however, its deputies refused to attend parliamentary sessions). Euzkadiko Ezkerra (EE, Basque Left), the political wing of a more moderate but still violent Basque terrorist group, ETA politico-militar, got 1 seat, as did the Unión Nacional (National Union), a federation of neofascist groups. The nonextremist regionalist Partido Socialista de Andalucia (PSA, Socialist Party of Andalucia), an affiliate of the PSOE, won 5 seats, joining the nonextremist Catalan and Basque regionalist parties, the CiU and the PNV. The AP lost almost half of its representation in the Congress.

Even more significant than these phenomena was the altered appearance of the UCD. The party had begun to move to the right, a shift that eventually would lead to Adolfo Suárez's resignation from the premiership and departure from the party, although the prime minister himself had helped to initiate the shift during the 1979 campaign. The electorate had always perceived the UCD to be more to the right than the party acknowledged. The party sought to project a centrist image and to occupy a political space that enclosed the "civilized right" and the non-Marxist, social democratic left. It sought the Catholic vote but eschewed any suggestion of confessionalism, a tactic made possible in part by the attitude of the hierarchy of the Spanish Catholic church, which maintained a low political profile in the earlier electoral outings. Through the voice of the Catholic Episcopal Conference, the church was not so quiet in the 1979 campaign, and whereas the church did not endorse the UCD (or the AP, for that matter), it did warn against those parties whose "commitments affect religious values or fundamental rights." The bishops' pronouncement went on to say: "We are especially concerned about proposals for the legalization of abortion, for divorce, and for educational reform that might limit the right of parents to choose the proper kind of education for their children."[1] The bishops' targets were, of course, the PSOE and the PCE, and Suárez took common ground with the church in his televised speech on the final day of campaigning. He declared that his party offered the alternative of "Christian humanism" to "Marxist socialist materialism."[2]

Perhaps Suárez felt he could politically afford this overtly rightist, pro-Catholic appeal because the Socialist party had not yet made its momentous decision to eliminate the adjective "Marxist" from its self-definition. That action would not take place until the extraordinary congress of the PSOE in September 1979. The Communist party went to the polls in 1979 with Leninism already excised from its definition but it remained Marxist. Thus, Suárez tarred both parties in his plea for the support of good Christians. His strategy was successful. The UCD stayed in power; the PSOE remained in second place. The PCE merely held its own, and the AP (from which Catholic voters switched to the UCD) appeared moribund.

Its still official Marxism did not keep the Socialist party from succeeding in the local elections that took place on April 3, 1979, the first nationwide municipal elections since April 12, 1931. At stake were 69,613 town and parish council seats in 8,041 municipalities. The UCD put up candidates in almost all of the constituencies, the PSOE in fewer than half of them. The UCD won 29,614 of the seats; the PSOE, 12,220; and the PCE, 3,608. The remaining seats were divided among nine other parties plus 14,817 independent representatives.

The PSOE received fewer than half the seats taken by the UCD, but the location of these seats gave the Socialists an enormous boost. Madrid, Málaga, Barcelona, Valencia, Zaragoza, and Gerona elected Socialist majorities, and Seville voted Socialist as well, its votes going primarily to the Socialist Party of Andalucia. In short, the majority of the great population centers (except Bilbao in the Basque provinces) voted for the PSOE. These victories were the first in a series that would take the PSOE to both national and local power in 1982 and 1983, and they were won primarily at the expense of the party's major rival, the UCD.

THE UCD IN TROUBLE

Between 1979 and 1982 the Socialists and their increasingly popular leader, Felipe González, gained stature and strength after ridding themselves of what González considered to be an outdated Marxist identity and a major impediment to electoral success. But the PSOE grew in importance not so much because it continued to best the UCD in electoral competition but because the UCD's stature and strength were gradually weakened either by the action of other parties—regionalist parties primarily—or by the UCD's own self-inflicted wounds.

By the spring of 1980 the steps prescribed in article 151 of the constitution for the rapid path of autonomy had been fulfilled in the three Basque provinces, Vizcaya, Guipúzcoa, and Álava (Navarre chose to become an autonomous region unto itself), and in all four of the Catalan provinces. On March 9, 1980, elections were held to the legislature of Euzkadi (the Basque name for the new Basque region), and similar elections were held in Catalonia on March 20. In Euzkadi, regionalist parties won first, second, and fourth places in the elections. The PSOE came in third with 14 percent of the votes, but the UCD received only 8.4 percent. In Catalonia the regionalist CiU won the plurality with 28 percent of the vote, followed by the PSOE with 23 percent. The UCD (with its Catalan affiliate) was fourth with only 11 percent. The elections to the legislature in newly autonomous Galicia took place eighteen months later, on October 20, 1981. The AP won the plurality with 34 percent of the vote, followed closely by the UCD with 31 percent. The most devastating blow to the position and pride of the UCD was delivered by the PSOE in the elections to the legislature of autonomous Andalucia, held on May 23, 1982. The PSOE overwhelmed all the other parties, winning 52 percent of the vote and 66 seats out of 109. The nearest competitor, the AP, won 17 percent and 17 seats. The UCD received a little over 11 percent and 14 seats. Only the PCE performed worse, with 8 percent and 8 seats. The defeat of the UCD in Andalucia came when the party was struggling in Madrid to keep itself from flying apart. Andalucia and Galicia are among the poorest, least literate, most backward parts of Spain, in many ways almost Third World in their plight. Euzkadi and Catalonia are the richest, most progressive, most educated regions of Spain, comparable in income and lifestyle to the most advanced parts of Western Europe. The rejection of the UCD by regions as dissimilar as these reflects the fragmented image that the party was projecting by the spring of 1982.

The first signs of disintegration had appeared in 1979, when the UCD's constituent elements began to chafe. Some believe the UCD was a cynical, opportunistic creature of that part of the political elite that had served Franco but was ready to accommodate itself to democracy in order to maintain power. Others believe that the UCD was the expression of truly progressive men and women who wanted Spain to make the transition to democracy as peacefully and painlessly as possible. Whatever the case, the UCD was truly the party of the transition. Once the constitution of 1978 had come into force and the first Cortes had been elected in 1979, the centripetal force that had kept the pieces of the UCD together had dissolved. The goals that had magnetized the diverse parts—Liberals, Social Democrats, and Christian Democrats, primarily—between 1977 and 1979 had been reached, and their natural incompatibilities emerged.

The UCD had been created from the top down by those already in power. For these men (and a few women), the UCD and the state were synonymous. Most of the UCD philosophy had come out of Francoism, under which the state and the caudillo were one. The automatic identification of incumbent with uncontested power had become almost second nature to UCD members. The notion that the apparatus of the state could some day be controlled by another party was not fully comprehensible to the UCD elite, and it never fully learned how to fight politically because it never believed that it would need to. The "center" with which the party identified appeared sacred and seemingly eternal, verified for the party by the results of the 1979 elections. In some ways, the barons of the UCD (as its leaders were perceptively called) were like the *hidalgos* of the sixteenth century, for whom work was beneath contempt. To the political hidalgos of the UCD, work, in the form of grubby, sweaty electioneering, was alien, and the tailored suits and silk ties of the UCD elite contrasted tellingly with the corduroy pants and pullover sweater of a tieless Felipe González. The UCD had not built an effective, bureaucratized, and institutionalized grass-roots party structure. The UCD went to the hustings primarily through personalities, as did the PSOE and the PCE, but the parties on the left had been created from the bottom up by men and women outside the halls of power, and the grass-roots infrastructure had been carefully built and tended. When those at the top of the UCD began to fight and fall out among themselves, the party fragmented, for it had almost no existence apart from its founding fathers.

The political demise of Adolfo Suárez within the UCD paralleled the disintegration of the party itself. A detailed account of his loss of power amidst personal and ideological intraparty feuds awaits definitive scholarship based on sources that are as yet unavailable. Most likely, his power failed to survive the transition to democracy because the elements that made up the federation of the UCD no longer felt constrained to take his discipline. His colleagues' fears that the failure to create a democratic constitution and to elect a government under its provisions could lead to the reappearance of dictatorship contributed mightily to Suárez's authority and power. His peers subordinated their own ambitions and ideological commitments to the larger task of rebuilding Spanish democracy. Moreover, Suárez's intimacy with Juan Carlos (who kept the army in control) made opposition to the prime minister a risky undertaking. Once his fellow party members felt that the new political system was relatively safe from military uprising and from leftist domination (demonstrated in the ballots of 1979), they began to express their true feelings. Some say that Suárez's personality was not attuned enough to the free-for-all of hands-on democratic politics nor dynamic enough to sustain the interest of the average Spaniard once the Suárez/democracy fascination had lost its novelty. Spaniards respond enthusiastically to strong personalities, particularly those that link style with easy grace—the combination epitomized by Felipe González, for example.

By late 1980 Suárez realized that his effectiveness had come to an end and believed that his party was moving too far to the right for comfort. On January 29, 1981, at the party conference in Mallorca, Suárez resigned as prime minister, urging, in his address to the delegates, that the UCD remain a centrist party, and stressing that to do otherwise would betray the voters' confidence. He declared that a move to the right would fundamentally alter the character of the party. The conferees responded by choosing Leopoldo Calvo Sotelo, a conservative centrist, as its nominee for prime minister. The party presidency, formerly held by Suárez, went to Agustín Rodríguez Sahagún, Suárez's brother-in-law and a dedicated centrist.

THE CRISIS OF FEBRUARY 1981

Juan Carlos nominated Calvo Sotelo for the premiership. Voting for confirmation took place in the Congress on February 10, 1981, but Calvo failed to receive the necessary majority on the first balloting. The second round was scheduled for February 23, 1981, but as voting was in progress, all hell broke loose. Antonio Tejero Molina, a lieutenant colonel in the Civil Guard, burst armed onto the floor of the Congress, accompanied by other armed guardsmen. Together they held the entire body of representatives hostage, eventually freeing the female deputies. A second conspirator, captain-general of the military region of Valencia General Jaime Milans del Bosch, simultaneously mobilized the units under his command and placed Valencia under martial law. In Madrid a third conspirator, General Alfonso Armado Comyn, who had tutored the young Juan Carlos in the 1950s and 1960s and who had been a close friend of the prince, sought to implicate the king in the plot. Armado telephoned Juan Carlos and offered to appear at the palace to help the sovereign arrive at a decision about the coup. The plan of Tejero, Milans, and Armado was to convert Juan Carlos to their cause, with his approval overthrow the government, and set up an authoritarian monarchy under the protection of the armed forces. The plan failed primarily—perhaps exclusively—because Juan Carlos refused to take part. He worked throughout the night of February 23 to rally military officers loyal to the crown and ordered the conspirators to desist. At 1 A.M. on February 24 he spoke to the nation on television in an address taped earlier in the evening. The king urged the people to have trust and remain calm and informed them that the constitution would be honored. By a little past dawn on February 24, the coup was over. The majority of the military stayed loyal to the king, and the king stayed loyal to the constitution. In this author's opinion, the king behaved magnificently. His commitment to democracy was total, and his behavior was in the great heroic tradition. These events showed, however, how vulnerable Spain still was to military insurrection and how fragile freedom remained. The military stayed loyal to the king personally, not to the system, and the decision of one man could have returned the country to dictatorship. The euphoria about the end of the transition had been premature.

Perhaps we will never know how deeply the conspiracy extended into the armed forces and into the social, economic, and ecclesiastical elite, nor just how much information—if any—the government had of the plot. The Socialists were particularly severe in insinuating that the UCD ministers could not have been caught totally by surprise, as the PSOE leaders, without access to the state intelligence network available to the government, had already deduced that something was brewing. Moreover, an enigmatic statement Suárez had made in his televised farewell address to the nation upon resigning was replayed in the people's minds after the aborted coup. "I am going because I do not want democracy to be a little parenthesis in the history of Spain." On the day following the most dangerous and traumatic event since the assassination of Carrero Blanco in December 1973, Suárez went on his planned holiday as if nothing had happened. We will not speculate here. Many questions remain unanswered, questions that go back even earlier than F-23 (February 23, 1981), as the event is now referred to in Spain. In November 1978, the month before the constitution was ratified in referendum, the same Lt. Colonel Tejero, a police captain named Ricardo Sáenz, and several others had been arrested for conspiracy to overthrow the government. Eighteen months later, Tejero was sentenced by military court to seven months in prison and Sáenz to six. For the military tribunal, the price for conspiracy in Spain was obviously cut-rate.

When the F-23 conspirators were finally sentenced in June 1982, after military trials during which the highest ranking accused sat on magnificent high-backed chairs upholstered in red velvet, the three central plotters—Tejero, Comyn, and Milans—were each sentenced to thirty years in prison and expelled from service without pay. But the sentences given to the remaining twenty-nine military conspirators, plus one civilian, were so light that they caused a national uproar and led Calvo Sotelo to appeal the sentences to the civilian Supreme Court.

DISINTEGRATION OF THE UCD

For a brief period after the attempted coup, the various groups within the UCD huddled for self-protection and rallied around Calvo Sotelo who, after the interruption on February 23–24, had finally been elected prime minister. The moratorium on infighting quickly passed, however. The catalyst that triggered the final break-up of the UCD was the conflict that swirled around the divorce bill sponsored by Francisco Fernández Ordóñez, the minister of justice and the leader of the social democratic left wing of the party.

It may be difficult for an outsider to appreciate the passion that surrounded the divorce issue in traditionally Catholic Spain. Not only did divorce profoundly affect the family, the most sacred social institution in Spain, it also undermined the supremacy of the male in what might be the most patriarchal society in Western Europe, patriarchal in terms of male dominance and of the male mystique captured in the word *machismo*. Divorce symbolized the newly liberated, permissive, open post-Franco society, embraced by many, excoriated by many. Moreover, in a society in which illegality as defined by the state and sin as defined by the church had often been synonymous, divorce during the Franco regime was not only sinful but also illegal. The divorce bill was approved in the Congress and then went to the Senate, where it was amended to allow a judge to deny a divorce if either party claimed that the divorce would cause undue suffering because of age, health or length of marriage. The Senate's version would have emasculated the bill, and the amendment was voted down after the bill returned to the Congress for final disposition. The UCD broke ranks on the vote, ignoring a warning from prime minister Calvo Sotelo not to do so. With PSOE, PCE, and the rebel UCD votes the bill became law on July 20, 1981, amidst outcries from the church and from its mouthpieces in the Cortes, primarily the AP and the Christian democratic right wing of the UCD, that Spain and the family were on the road to perdition.

After the passage of the divorce bill the UCD relentlessly tore itself apart in a struggle for control between the supporters of Calvo Sotelo, who favored a conservative policy that would pull the party further to the right, and the supporters of Suárez, who sought to hold firm at the center. On July 25, 1981, thirty-nine UCD deputies from the Christian democratic wing signed a letter to party president Sahagún decrying the party's drift to the left, citing the divorce bill as primary evidence. A "pacification" document presented by Sahagún the following September defining the UCD as a "reformist, progressive, center party" achieved none of its conciliatory goals. Already in August Fernández Ordóñez had resigned as minister of justice and in November, after Sahagún's "pacification" had failed, he abandoned the UCD accompanied by eight other deputies. Their attempt to form a new social democratic parliamentary group in Congress failed, and they were forced to join the mixed group of unaffiliated deputies. In that same November three more deputies left the party to join the AP, and Sahagún resigned as the UCD's president. The party presidency went to Prime Minister Calvo Sotelo. Adolfo Suárez then announced that he too might leave the party. The exodus continued until by early January UCD membership in the Congress had fallen to 150 deputies.

In late March 1982, Fernández Ordóñez created a new party, the social democratic Partido Acción Democrático (PAD, Democratic Action Party). In July of 1982, Antonio Garrigues Walker abandoned the UCD and formed the Partido Democrático Liberal (PDL, Liberal Democratic Party); Oscar Alzaga left the UCD to form the conservative Christian democratic Partido Democrático Popular (PDP, Popular Democratic Party); and Calvo Sotelo resigned the UCD party presidency. The position went not to Suárez but to Landelino Lavilla, the majority leader in the Congress and a member of the Christian democratic wing of the party. Finally, on July 29, 1982, Adolfo Suárez, after failing to regain control of the UCD, resigned from the party he had created and announced that he was forming a new one, the Centro Democrático Social (CDS, Democratic and Social Center). By August 1982, UCD membership in Congress had fallen to 122 deputies. With the party's left and right wings now gone and the center contested by the CDS, the UCD had become a vaguely centrist party under the control of conservatives located at various degrees right of center. The once powerful party had become an amorphous remnant totally incapable of political leadership. Spain could not endure seven months of governmental inaction awaiting the expiration of the legislative mandate in March 1983. On August 27, 1982, Juan Carlos dissolved the Cortes and called for new elections to take place the following October.

SWING TO THE LEFT

The pre-electoral polls had predicted that the PSOE woud be victorious, but the final tally after the election of October 28, 1982, even if expected, was almost inconceivable for Spain. The turnout was 78.8 percent of the 26,517,393 registered voters, and the abstention rate was lower than in any previous electoral contest or referendum. The PSOE won 202 out of the 350 seats in the Congress, giving it an absolute majority. The AP won the second highest number with 106. The next closest party, the UCD, won only 13 (compared to 168 in

Table 10.1
Results of the 1979 and 1982 Elections

Political Party	Votes in 1982	Seats in Congress 1982	1979
PSOE/PSC-POE	10,127,392	202	121
AP/AP-PDP	5,543,107	106	9
UCD	1,425,093	12	168
CiU	772,726	12	8
PNV	395,656	8	7
PCE-PSUC	844,976	4	23
CDS	600,842	2	--
HB	210,601	2	3
ERC	138,116	1	1
EE	100,326	1	1
Independents and others	648, 346	0	9

Source: Keesing's Contemporary Archives
(Bath, England: Keesing's Publications)
24 (March 1983): 32012.

1979). Suárez's new party came in seventh with 2 seats. For the total breakdown of votes, see Table 10.1.

Several comments should be made about the electoral results. The extremist regional parties were weaker in 1982 than when they first appeared in 1979. The HB lost a seat, giving it only 2, and the EE managed only to hold on to the single seat it had. By contrast, moderate regionalist parties, the CiU and the PNV, gained strength, the former going from 8 to 12 seats, the latter from 7 to 8. The PCE (allied for the election with its Catalan counterpart, the PSUC) was almost wiped out at the national level, falling from 23 seats in 1979 to 4 in 1982.

The political posture of the Spaniards demonstrated in the national elections in 1982 was maintained in the municipal and autonomous region elections held throughout Spain on May 8, 1983. Out of the 57,908 municipal council seats contested, the PSOE won 21,545; the AP (in alliance with the PDP and the Liberals) won the second largest number, 16,521. The closest rival, the PCE, won only 2,462. In the 52 provincial capitals (including Ceuta and Melilla), the PSOE won control in 38, the AP in 10, the PNV in 3, and the PCE won in Cordoba. In the 13 autonomous regions in which elections were held the PSOE won 389 out of a total of 764 legislative seats; the AP won the second largest number, 272. The PCE won 27; the CDS, 8; followed by the PDL with 2. All other parties and independents won 66. In an unprecedented situation for Western Europe, a socialist party was in the majority at every level of government: national, regional, provincial, and municipal.

The results of the 1982 national elections and their reaffirmation in the regional and municipal elections in 1983 offer an optimistic prognosis for Spanish democracy. In only their second national elections under the new constitution and after fewer than seven years from the beginning of the transition to democracy, the relatively politically unpracticed Spaniards had sufficient faith in their political system and in the platforms of their major parties to reject the rightist incumbent and elect into office the strongest party on the left, a transition that was accomplished without a breakdown of the democratic process. (It took the supposedly more politically sophisticated and experienced French thirty-six years, from 1945 to 1981, to do the same thing, and for the first time since the creation of their republic in 1946, the Italians have a socialist government created in the summer of 1983, not as the result of direct electoral mandate, as in Spain and France, however, but as the consequence of cabinet reshuffling.) In Spain, the center has disappeared, the PSOE controls the government, and the AP, which seemed on its way to extinction after the 1979 elections, has become the opposition.

After public opinion polls indicated that the PSOE's dazzling sweep to power in Andalucia in May 1982 would probably be duplicated at the next national elections, magazines, newspapers, and scholarly journals were filled with articles written by men and women loyal to the political center who feared the possible polarization of Spanish politics that could occur as a result of the October elections. These authors did not consider themselves to be alarmists when they urged their fellow Spaniards to reembrace the center and avoid a move either to the right (to the AP) or to the left (to the PSOE or PCE). They were acutely aware of the history of the Second Republic, in which the hatred between the two poles erupted from the left in 1934 and then from the right in 1936. A repeat of these confrontations had to be prevented, and the writers believed that only a rigorous stance at the center, almost an act of will and self-discipline, would avert disaster. Moreover, they believed that the center deserved to be rewarded and perpetuated because of its extraordinary accomplishments: the transition to democracy culminating in the constitution of 1978 and the elections of 1979.

These warnings notwithstanding, the electorate rejected the center and moved toward the left and toward the right. The Spaniards repudiated the ignominious UCD rump. The party's ideological identification in the election of 1982 was not cut from whole cloth but was pieced together out of what was left after the constituent parts had pulled away. The electorate rejected even more adamantly the new centrist party created by Adolfo Suárez, which appeared to be more the dull reflection of politics past than the bright image of politics to come. Suárez looked like the old man of politics, and whereas in the 1970s he had been a paladin, in 1982 he seemed an opportunist. The AP, particularly after the defection of its right wing, appeared by contrast as a muscular yet allegiant conservative alternative, vigorously, if not abrasively, championed by Manuel Fraga Iribarne—seen by many to be a stalwart and worthy opponent of Felipe González.

At the national level, Spain has for all practical purposes become a two-party system, divided between Left and Right. The essential difference between Spain in 1983 and Spain during the Second Republic lies in the nature of the two parties that speak for the majority and the minority. Both the PSOE and the AP have declared that they accept the system and will play by the democratic rules of politics. The AP had been tarred earlier by antisystem elements, but most of these defected to parties further to the right, moving the AP automatically toward the center. The PSOE has disavowed its revolutionary Marxist ideology, moving this party toward the center as well. Thus Left and Right have become in reality center Left and center Right, and even if Spain has not yet psychologically embraced the concept of loyal opposition that the British follow, the foundation of such behavior is perhaps being laid down at the present time. The first electoral test for Spanish democracy took place in 1982 when the artificial center was demolished and the nation split into a traditional Left-Right division. The country gave its support to the Left, and the Right accepted the verdict of the people. The next test will occur when the people turn toward the Right and place the Left in opposition. If the Right then comports itself in office as responsibly as the Left is behaving now and the Left accepts the Right with the same tolerance as the Right now accepts the Left, then perhaps the transition will have finally come to an end and democracy will be safe in Spain.

NOTES

1. *Informaciones,* February 9, 1979, p. 31.
2. *Informaciones,* February 28, 1979, p. 3.

11

Violence and Terrorism

Spain in the 1980s has the best opportunity in its history for good government. The people seem ready; the socioeconomic signs are propitious, despite the current problems of inflation and unemployment that affect not just Spain but the whole world; and the quality of politicians appears high. Unfortunately, the statistics of violence intrude.

Terrorism comes primarily from the Left and within the Left mostly from among the Basques. Terrorism from the Right is dispersed throughout the nation. The ETA is the most notorious of the groups on the left and the one best known outside of Spain, but until December 1982, the mysterious GRAPO, an acronym for the First of October Anti-Fascist Resistance Group, also maintained a deadly presence. In the first week of December, the last of its remaining original members not in captivity was gunned down by the police in Barcelona. The organization may not be permanently finished, however. It has died before and, like the phoenix, has risen again.

On the Right are over a dozen groups, some of them quite small. The most violent is the Frente de la Juventud (Youth Front), made up of about 150 activists. The founders split away from Fuerza Nueva (New Force), the right-wing party of Blas Piñar that won no seats in the 1982 elections and has since disbanded. The most chilling fact about the Youth Front (if one can compare degrees of cold-bloodedness) is the age of many of its soldiers. "Of the forty-two youngsters who joined the Nazi organization in the first three months of 1982, two were under fourteen years of age, fourteen had not yet turned fifteen, and ten were about to celebrate their sixteenth birthday."[1] Without doubt the most exotically named group on the right is the Guerrilleros de Cristo Rey, the Guerrilla Fighters of Christ the King (whose motto could easily be "Kill a Commie for Christ").

The Guerrillas are God's militant laymen. He also has professionals among the ranks of the terrorists. It is estimated that approximately 3 percent of Basque priests are sympathizers or supporters of the ETA.[2] Most do not carry arms or directly take part in the violence, but many are certainly accomplices to mayhem, murder, and kidnapping. The pro-ETA clergy aid the terrorists by maintaining hideouts and places of refuge, furnishing locations for arsenals, and by lending monasteries, convents, sacristies, and churches for clandestine meetings. They make propaganda at public religious ceremonies like weddings and funerals. Some, however, have given up the cassock to wear the wardrobe of the ETA militant soldiers, and of these a few have been arrested, one for killing a retired Civil Guardsman. The most notorious of all the outlaw priests was Eustaquio Mendizábal, who was shot and killed by the police in 1973.

The Basques are the most religious people in Spain, and they produce a larger number of priests per capita than any other region of the country. In 1979, non-Basque Spain produced 3.2 priests per 1,000 inhabitants; in Euzkadi the percentage was 5.2, and in Navarre, 7.1. Among these devout men, however, are some who, like the Guerrillas for Christ the King on the right, also kill for God. They rationalize their conversion to bloodshed by declaring that there is a state of war between Euzkadi and the rest of Spain. They believe that they are not helping the ETA but are instead aiding an occupied people, just as the members of the underground in Europe during World War II helped their fellow citizens against the Nazis. In their own minds, the Basque priests who have faith in the ETA are not monsters but heroes.

Since 1970 approximately 400 people have died violently at the hands of political assassins. From November 1977 to February 1983, 38 military officers lost their lives to left-wing terrorists. From June 1979 to July 1982, 86 people, all ordinary citizens, were "sentenced" and "executed" by the ETA after having been accused of informing the police.[3] On the other side of the political spectrum right-wing terrorists killed 46 men and women between September 1979 and December 1981.[4]

The breakdown for 1977 to 1982 shows a net increase in terrorist killings. In 1977, 30 people throughout Spain were killed by terrorists; in 1978 the number rose to 99 (67 in the Basque region) and in 1979 to 123 (66 in the Basque region). In 1980, 126 people lost their lives through terrorism, with 85 deaths attributed to the ETA and 33 to various other groups on the extreme right and the extreme left (the remaining 6 were uncredited). In 1981, the killings dropped to 49 people; 31 of the deaths took place in the Basque provinces.[5] In addition to killings, the ETA kidnapped 45 men and 1 woman for ransom between 1970 and 1982. Three victims were assassinated; and of the 43 released by their abductors, many suffer permanent physical injury and even more bear permanent psychological scars.[6]

The ETA is no longer a single organization. It has split into the ETA militar (military), which is committed totally to revolution, violence, and bloodshed, and the ETA político-militar (political-military), which is more moderate and more willing to negotiate and take part in the political process, but still prepared to kill for its cause. For example, it was the ETA p-m that set off the chain of bombings at the beach resorts on the Spanish Mediterranean coast in June and July 1979, and on July 29, 1979, the ETA p-m claimed responsibility for the bombings in the two largest railway stations in Madrid and in the nation's largest and busiest airport at Barajas outside the capital. Five people were killed, including a West German tourist.

The ETA has said that it originally resorted to violence as the only way to be heard by Franco, who had turned deaf ears to the supplications and demands of the Basque people. Many observers believed that once Franco was dead the unfortunate plight of the Basques (and of other repressed Spanish peoples like the Catalans and the Galicians) would at last be alleviated. Hope for a peaceful solution increased when the men who guided the transition to democracy, in particular King Juan Carlos and Adolfo Suárez, acknowledged the legitimacy of regionalist claims. Autonomy began to be actualized first through pre-autonomy decrees issued by the monarch, then through provisions for autonomy written into the constitution, and finally through the creation of regional legislatures and governments by elections that took place beginning in the spring of 1980. The violence of the ETA did not subside, however. On the contrary, terrorism increased, particularly on the eve of elections and referenda. The ETA revealed through bloodshed its opposition to any political process that took place under the auspices of the national government and that would legitimize the Spanish state. It became apparent that the ETA, and in particular the ETA militar, would settle for nothing short of independence for Euzkadi followed by a Marxist revolution within the new state.

In the beginning the ETA had aimed its violence primarily at the hated symbols of Spanish national sovereignty: the police, the army, and above all the Civil Guard that patrols the provinces. As its campaign grew more fanatical, more ambitious, and more costly, the ETA unleashed violence against fellow Basques. Sophisticated modern weaponry purchased in the international black market of arms and munitions is enormously expensive, and money had to be found. Kidnappings for ransom, especially of Basque industrialists and entrepreneurs, reached epidemic proportions, but extortion became even more widespread, amounting to nothing less than protection money gouged out of ordinary citizens. The major sources of the "revolutionary tax" (*impuesto revolucionario*), as the money is called by the terrorists, were doctors and other professionals who earned large incomes,[7] but as time went on and expenses increased the "tax collectors" began to include humble folk as well, particularly small shopkeepers and bar and cafe owners, people dependent upon the public for their livelihood.[8] Those who refused to donate to the cause of revolution ran the risk of losing their lives, having their businesses boycotted, or their premises destroyed or damaged. Eventually the ETA terrorists expanded their extortion from individuals to large commercial enterprises, especially banks.[9] On April 23, 1982, members of the boards of directors of the Banks of Vizcaya, Santander, Hispano-Americano, and Guipuzcoana received letters from the ETA militar demanding a total of 1,000 million pesetas. Banks that refused to come up with the money risked being bombed.

Panic has been spread among the rest of the Basque population by labeling as *chivato* (goat) anyone who has contact with the police, thus frightening away even those citizens who have legitimate complaints unassociated with terrorism. Law enforcement and the judicial process have thereby been undermined, and the entire social, economic, and political infrastructure of the system is gradually eroding in the Basque provinces. Professionals such as doctors and lawyers are leaving the region. Owners are abandoning their houses, particularly those located in the remote countryside. Businesses are closing their doors; foreign investment is drying up; and tourism has already died in parts of Euzkadi.

The ETA terrorists have seemingly slipped into collective insanity. They are destroying the region they claim to love above all else, and their activity runs the risk of provoking a military intervention in the national political process that would not only bring down democracy but would destroy Euzkadi as well. The right-wing extremists in the armed forces and their sympathizers among the civilian elite would show no mercy in suppressing the Basques. Moreover, the killing of innocent people by the ETA would offer the perfect rationale for the armed forces of the state to kill innocent Basques. If unleashed, the army, the police, and the Civil Guards would be far more powerful than even the most powerful terrorist group.

The vast majority of the Basque people abhor the violence; moreover, the Marxist revolution sought by the ETA extremists would destroy the capitalist economy of the Basque region (along with Catalonia, the richest in Spain), most of whose citizens are comfortably bourgeois. Yet the Basque people are caught in a terrible dilemma. Fear prevents most of them from acting against the ETA, and a crisis of conscience prevents the rest from condemning the ETA outright. At the beginning the members of the ETA were willing to risk their lives in order to defend the Basque language, culture, and ancient fueros. The ETA militants were heroes who have now turned into criminals. Some people call the ETA the Basque mafia, but the Basque people cannot forget what the group once stood for nor what it was once willing to die for. Perhaps the words of Marenchu Echeverría express it best. Echeverría was the deputy mayor of Tolosa in the province of Guipúzcoa and the daughter of a Loyalist who fled to exile during the Civil War and finally returned to Spain in 1977. She herself had been active in creating the *ikastolas,* the underground schools designed to keep the Basque language and Basque nationalism alive during the Franco regime. The schools now operate openly and are demanding their share of public funding from the national government.

> We will have to go after them [the ETA] with our own police force, and I'll be in favor of jailing and bringing them to trial. . . . But I could never bring myself to inform on them, not now, not ever, not for any amount of money. It just isn't something I could do after all these years.[10]

NOTES

1. *Cambio 16,* August 30, 1982, p. 15.
2. *Cambio 16,* June 20, 1983, pp. 20–26.
3. *Cambio 16,* August 23, 1982, p. 18.
4. *Cambio 16,* August 30, 1982, p. 15.
5. *Keesing's Contemporary Archives,* 1977–1982.
6. *Cambio 16,* December 27, 1982, p. 27.
7. *Cambio 16,* January 17, 1983, p. 15.
8. *Cambio 16,* August 2, 1982, pp. 16–20.
9. *Cambio 16,* February 14, 1983, pp. 16–21.
10. *International Herald Tribune,* August 6, 1979, p. 2.

Part 4
The Socioeconomic Context

12

The Economy

In 1980, Spanish economist Juan Velarde Fuertes speculated about the proletarianization of the Spanish middle class. In the three years that have passed since he voiced his concern, the economic situation in Spain has worsened, making his conjecture seem more plausible now than it was then. Paradoxically, Spain did not start to develop a middle class until the 1960s, and assuming that building a solid middle class is the objective of most developing nations, the proletarianization of Spain would amount to the collapse of the goal even before the majority of Spanish citizens had it in sight. Until the 1960s Spain was a poor country, with 48 percent of its population living from agriculture, often at the subsistence level. The transformation of the country in the past quarter of a century from penury to prosperity and from agriculture to industry has been nothing short of phenomenal, and the Spanish "miracle" joins the Italian and the German "miracles" as one of the major Western European economic events of the post–World War II era. The Spanish miracle is now in jeopardy. The threat to the Spanish economy was catalyzed by the action of the oil-producing cartel in the mid-1970s, but it has been exacerbated in Spain by conditions of Spain's own making.

THE TRADITION OF AUTARKY

A brief digression is necessary to put the situation into historical perspective. The Industrial Revolution did not reach Spain until the 1960s. There had been large-scale manufac-

turing in Spain since the last century, and certain areas of
the country were even then classified as industrial: Catalonia
with textiles and the Basque provinces with heavy industry
(in part fueled by coal from Asturias). The rest of the country
was agricultural, the land worked for the most part by a
depressed peasantry. The largest commercial farmers were
the aristocratic absentee wheat growers of Castile, who, together with the Basque and Catalan industrial elite, successfully
pressured the state to protect their interests with tariffs that
by the early twentieth century were the highest in Europe.
Import duties kept out not only the goods and services that
might have competed against those of the protected Spanish
oligarchy but also the technology and mentality that might
have transformed the essentially conservative, provincial Malthusian Spanish society into a modern, progressive one.[1] Spain
became a tight little island effectively cut off from the rest
of the then developing Western world. There was some foreign
investment in Spain, primarily in railroads, public utilities,
and mining, but the Spanish laws that allowed foreign investors
to bring money into Spain also allowed them to take out
profits earned within the country. They were not compelled
to reinvest in the Spanish economy; instead they were compelled to purchase domestic products, entrenching protectionism and enriching the Spanish elite. By contrast, the
Spanish masses profited very little from foreign investors,
who seemed like state-sponsored carpetbaggers allowed into
the country to reap their profits from essential services that
the Spanish elite could not or would not itself supply and
then ushered out of the country as if their presence would
contaminate Spanish life. Isolation and self-sufficiency, a kind
of spiritual and material autarky, seemed to be the ideal of
those who ruled Spain, even if the price of national aloofness
was a retrograde society.

Isolation by Choice

During the regime of Primo de Rivera, the Spanish state
itself began to play a larger role in the pursuit of autarky.
The state took over sectors formerly developed by foreign

entrepreneurs, particularly investing in essential infrastructural development. This should not be interpreted as an indication of sudden concern for the welfare of the Spanish masses. The state was the public face of Spain's ruling elite, and its decision to move into large-scale public enterprise reflected the oligarchy's desire to use public monies to finance activity too risky for private capital. Primo initiated an ambitious program of public works: road building, river navigation, irrigation, and land reclamation. He set up semiofficial banks to encourage investment in projects considered to be in the national interest. He created the Compañía Arrendataria del Monopolio de Petróleos (CAMPSA, Regulatory Company of Petroleum Monopoly) as a state concession to regulate the petroleum industry and to put into the national coffers the profits that had been going to foreign investors. Under Primo the state also became the majority stockholder of what later would be named Iberia, an international airline originally created by amalgamating several smaller firms.

Given a ruling elite that included both the industrial oligarchy of Catalonia and the Basque provinces and the landed aristocracy of Andalucia and Castile, it is not surprising that in his urge to transform Spain Primo left the anachronistic system of land tenure untouched. The *minifundio* was the small plot of land typical of northern Spain (with the exception of certain regions of Aragon, Catalonia, and the province of Salamanca); at its most extreme, in Galicia, holdings of less than 20 ha (49.4 acres) were common. This acreage was often fragmented into a dozen noncontiguous pieces, requiring the farmers to move from plot to plot scattered about the countryside and making the use of modern machinery and technology almost impossible. Even where the soil was rich it could not yield at maximum productivity.

The *latifundio* was the large, often giant-sized holding characteristic of southern Spain—particularly Andalucia, Extremadura, and La Mancha, where 500 ha (1,235 acres) per family was not uncommon, and where the Duke of Medinaceli, for example, owned 30,906 ha (76,338 acres). Most latifundios included large portions of grazing land unsuitable for farming. Even where the soil was rich and could be used for crops it was often farmed at less than maximum capacity, not because it did not lend itself to the techniques of large-scale production but because the owners were not interested in output greater than what could afford them a lifestyle of elegance and leisure—spent, ironically, not on the land but in Seville or Madrid or Paris or London. Land redistribution that might have allowed more families to own and till the land or a national agricultural policy that might have required the land to be used more productively were alternatives totally unacceptable to the landed gentry, one of the pillars of Primo's support at the beginning of the dictatorship.

During the short-lived Second Republic little was done to change the basic structure of the Spanish economy. Whether the republic might have accomplished more if its political forces had not spent their time tearing at one another is a moot question. During the Red Biennium, laws designed to redistribute land were passed, but the program had barely gotten off the ground when the government of the Black Biennium reversed the process. The Civil War broke out too soon after the Popular Front came into power for its land reform policies to be carried out.

The Civil War devastated Spain, and the economy was still in tatters twenty years later when the Stabilization Plan was inaugurated in 1959. Gabriel Jackson estimated that 580,000 people died as a direct result of the war.[2] Hugh Thomas put the figure at 600,000.[3] Ramón Tamames, a Spanish economist, goes further than either Jackson or Thomas in his appraisal of the total human and material cost of the war.[4] Tamames estimated that during the last months and immediately following the hostilities, approximately 300,000 men and women fled into exile, most of them in their prime, many of them skilled and educated. Comparing prewar to postwar demographic statistics, Tamames deduces that during the conflict the population fell another 500,000, more or less, because of the decline in the birthrate. He further calculates that 875,000 productive worker years were lost in prison. To this incredible human loss he adds the material devastation: (1) the equivalent of $575 million worth of gold spent by the republicans to finance the war; (2) the complete destruction of 250,000 dwellings and the partial destruction of 250,000 more out of a national total of approximately 6 million; (3) over 192 towns and cities more than 60 percent destroyed; (4) approximately 50 percent of all railway rolling stock and 30 percent of all merchant ships destroyed; (5) approximately 34.2 percent of cattle, 32.7 percent of sheep and goats, and 50.4 percent of pigs dead; (6) industrial production down approximately 31 percent, gross national income down by approximately 25.7 percent, and per capita income down by approximately 28.3 percent.

Isolation by Necessity

After World War II was over and Spain and the rest of Western Europe were ready to rebuild, the Franco regime was ostracized by the victorious Allies, refused admittance to the international political, social, and economic organizations that were being created, and ignored by the United States, whose largesse in the form of Marshall Plan aid put many European economies on their feet again. Franco embraced autarky because he had no other alternative, but in doing so he followed a Spanish tradition that was already half a century old.

At the beginning, Franco doubtless believed that his economic policy would be successful. Spain had survived in the past and would survive again. When, for example, the world depression came after 1929 Spain suffered less than most countries because of its isolation from the main currents of international trade and finance. Franco's economic policies were similar to those pursued by the leadership in prerepublican Spain, so he was on relatively familiar ground. Franco felt confident in his own economic decision making. He regulated domestic production, exports and imports, and subjected the latter to rigid licensing; he applied currency restrictions and adopted fluctuating exchange rates dependent upon the nature of the buyer and seller; he rationed consumer goods and fixed prices. He resorted to protectionism for certain economic activities and put the state into the business of postwar reconstruction for which private capital was either insufficient or unavailable.

Under Franco, the Instituto Nacional de Colonización (INC, National Institute of Land Development) replaced the Instituto de Reforma Agraria (IRA, Institute of Agrarian Reform) that had been created during the Red Biennium of the republic to oversee land redistribution. The INC was empowered to increase the area of cultivatable land—though not by expropriation—in order to feed a hungry nation. Eventually, the INC became the single largest landowner in Spain. Its role was to turn over to private ownership land acquired by the state. The breakup of the large estates, the latifundios, made even less sense in postwar Spain than it had during the republic, when political demands for land reform often ran counter to rational economic policy. If maximum agricultural output was the objective in postwar Spain, then large-scale farming was essential. The realities of economics and politics merged neatly here; the sanctity of private property was one of the pillars of Franco's belief system, and large landowners made up one of the pillars of the Franco regime. The Servicio de Concentración Parcelaria (SCP, the Land Parcel Consolidation Service) was formed to help consolidate the tiny separate holdings of the minifundios in order to increase production by the use of machinery. The Servicio Nacional de Trigo (SNT, National Wheat Service) came into being to regularize the distribution of wheat and, incidentally, to protect the pro-Franco wheat growers from the vissicitudes of the market; the SNT was given exclusive power to buy wheat from the primary producers, and could thus artificially determine what the going price of grain would be.

The state moved into industry through the Instituto Nacional de Industria (INI, National Institute of Industry). The INI was originally conceived to supplement private investment in those areas of particular national interest (armaments, for example) or in which an essential economic function might be insufficiently attractive to private capital. The institute soon went far beyond its original purpose and became involved in almost the entire gamut of economic activity: shipbuilding; automobile manufacturing; steel making; electricity; chemicals; cement; fertilizer. By 1960 it accounted for about 15 percent of all Spanish industrial investment. The INI became a power unto itself, wasteful and difficult to discipline. It perpetuated inefficient business enterprises whose low productivity was disproportionate to capital investment. Moreover, the resources of the INI came directly from the state, which resorted to the printing press when it got low on cash. These activities contributed mightily to the inflation that began to push up Spanish prices beyond competitive levels internationally, and domestically beyond the society's capacity to purchase.

Autarky failed to keep Spain apace with Western Europe. Foodstuffs and raw materials were still in short supply in the 1950s. The state-sponsored programs were not achieving the goals for which they had been created; their activities were out of sync and oftentimes counterproductive. Spain was stagnating; it had to break out of isolation or else join the ranks of what later came to be called the Third World. As Sima Lieberman writes: "The economics of the EEC [European Economic Community] were expanding; if Spain was to benefit from this expansion it had to shift rapidly away from policies of autarky and expand its trade with western Europe. The pace of economic advance in most of western Europe was progressively turning Spain into a more economically backward country."[5] When Franco adopted the familiar policy of autarky he could not have foreseen the qualitative socioeconomic change that would soon be taking place in Western Europe. In the past, Spain could be isolated, autarkic, and aloof but still stay within the limits of comparison to other members of the Western family of nations. That family was beginning to change so radically by the mid-1950s that Spain, looking backward and inward, was quickly falling behind. Spain was rapidly joining another family: the underdeveloped, preindustrial nations of the Third World.

SPAIN REJOINS THE WORLD

Spain's isolation ended in 1953 when Franco negotiated aid agreements with the United States and the concordat with the Vatican. The economic plight of the country began to be relieved somewhat by U.S. funds, but thoroughgoing economic change was needed for this pump priming to achieve permanent, positive results. In short, Spain needed a significant economic source to prime. A new economic policy had to be implemented, but Franco was out of his depth with anything more sophisticated than autarky. In February 1957, he made the momentous cabinet change that first brought into the government the young technocrats who were also members of the Opus Dei. These men, soon joined by other members of the Opus Dei society, authored the Stabilization Plan of 1959, designed to prepare Spain for entry into the outside world of trade and finance. It is said that Franco gave the aggressive innovators free reign, saying, "Hagan lo que les de la gana," properly translated, "Do whatever you wish." A more idiomatic translation would reveal Franco's impatience and frustration, forced into a policy that he did not like, that he knew he could not freely control once it was engaged, but that he could not avoid unless he were willing to settle for the pauperization of Spain: "Do whatever you damn well feel like doing."

The Stabilization Plan shut down the easy supply of money to entrepreneurs and increased the costs of goods and services essential to the people, slashing their purchasing power. It restricted the expansion of private bank credit by giving the minister of the interior the power to regulate credit and the discount practices of private banks. The plan raised the rates charged by the state-owned national railway, RENFE, increased the cost of telephone service, and upped the prices of lubricants, petroleum products, and tobacco. The peseta was devalued, and the plan set in motion the machinery that allowed foreign investment to come in. Foreign capital could comprise up to 50 percent of the total capital of a Spanish firm; with the approval of the cabinet foreign investment could exceed the 50 percent limitation. Furthermore, dividends and capital and asset appreciation generated by foreign investment could be repatriated.

Implementation of the Stabilization Plan caused an economic recession. Healthy firms were compelled to retrench when easy credit for new investment was not forthcoming;

many weak firms went out of business. Production fell; consumer demand decreased. New legislation made it easier to fire employees, and unemployment increased.[6] Just as the planners had envisaged, imports fell and exports rose as the cost of Spanish goods fell. The balance of payments improved significantly, providing Spain with foreign exchange. Lieberman writes:

> The Stabilization Plan of 1959 also stimulated economic growth through two major effects. By bringing the economy closer to a market system and by exposing Spanish firms to foreign competition, the Plan confronted domestic inefficient firms with the choice between increasing their productive efficiency or having to face probable business failure. It thus induced many firms to modernize their methods of production and to develop new products. By liberalizing foreign trade and by opening up the economy to foreign investment the Plan allowed Spain to benefit from its geographical proximity to the rapidly developing economy of western Europe.[7]

The plan readied Spain for the economic takeoff that occurred in the 1960s, but it would not take place in the free market economy recommended in the report from the International Bank of Reconstruction and Development. The report had been requested by the Spanish government, and the bank had sent its team of investigators to Spain in March 1961. Perhaps given Spain's history of state intervention in the economic process, the move to a free market economy would have been too severe a jolt for the country to endure. Moreover, the economic elite that supported Franco would not have tolerated the total exposure to competition that such an economy would have demanded. Finally, the men of the Opus Dei who were now in charge of Spain's economic regeneration would have lost a great deal of control if the free forces of the market and not governmental planning determined Spain's economic direction. In the place of a free market economy the Opus Dei technocrats borrowed a scheme that had worked successfully in France and adapted it to Spain: indicative planning, a cooperative effort between the state and private enterprise. The government set out the general scheme, which private enterprise was free either to follow or ignore. Following the plan brought great benefits, however, among them tax advantages, accelerated depreciation, special lines of credit, and subsidies. In order to encourage private investment in areas that the planners considered to be in need of development, the government designated certain national regions as Economic Poles and granted special benefits to private firms willing to operate within them. Development Poles were established in regions where a certain amount of industrialization already existed. Industrial Promotion Poles were created in regions with no or very little industrialization. *Polígonos de Decongesción Industrial* (Poles of Industrial Decongestion) were established to relieve the pressure built up in cities like Barcelona and Madrid. At the beginning of the 1970s, the concept of poles was expanded to integrate urban planning with industrial development in Metropolitan Zones exceeding 750,000 inhabitants and in Urban Zones of more than 250,000. Finally, the activities of the INI were curtailed and coordinated with the overall development plans. The INI was to concentrate on risky, long-range activities: providing aid for private firms in temporary financial difficulty until the firm was again stable; and protecting infant industries until they were strong enough to compete on their own.

Beginning in the 1960s, Spain's economic growth was spectacular. Table 12.1 gives Spanish growth rates compared to other western countries. In 1953, the Spanish gross domestic product was 14 percent of French GDP and 23 percent of that of Italy; by 1965, the Spanish GDP was 22 percent of France's and 39 percent of Italy's. In 1974, the figures were 23 and 40 percent. Using the date 1963 and the base figure 100, the net production per person employed in Spain rose from 100 in 1963 to 194 in 1971; comparable figures for Germany were 100 and 150; for Italy 100 and 153; for the Netherlands 100 and 163; and for Great Britain 100 and 134. From 1964 to 1972 Spanish wages rose an average of 287.9 percent. Per 1,000 people there were 190 passenger vehicles in use in Spain in 1979, compared to 70 in 1970; 35 commercial vehicles in use in 1979 compared to 22 in 1970; 280 telephones

Table 12.1
Annual GNP Growth Rate for Selected Western European Countries
1960-1968

Year	Spain	Germany	France	Italy	Belgium	UK
1960	2.7	8.8	7.1	6.3	5.5	4.7
1961	13.6	5.7	5.4	8.3	4.9	3.5
1962	11.3	4.4	6.8	6.3	5.6	1.3
1963	12.2	3.4	5.8	5.4	4.7	4.3
1964	13.3	6.8	6.6	2.9	6.9	5.3
1965	9.4	5.8	4.7	3.6	3.9	2.5
1966	9.3	2.5	5.5	5.9	2.8	2.0
1967	4.5	---	4.8	6.4	3.4	2.0
1968	6.0	7.5	4.2	5.7	3.8	2.8

Source: M. L. Ardura Calleja, "El sector industrial," in Juan Velarde Fuertes et al., La España en los años 70 (Madrid: Editorial Moneda y Crédito, 1973), p. 330.

in 1978, from 135 in 1970; 259 radios in 1976, compared to 228 in 1970; and 206 television sets in use in 1976, compared to 122 in 1970. Table 12.2 shows the growth of the gross industrial product from 1959 to 1971, and Table 12.3 compares the Spanish economy in 1960 to the economy in 1970.

THE ECONOMIC MIRACLE FALTERS

Statistics like those shown in Tables 12.2 and 12.3 make poignant Velarde Fuertes's suggestion that Spain might face the proletarianization of its middle class. A people new to comforts and luxury might be forced to cut back before they have even cut loose. Economic problems in Spain in the 1980s reflect the economic problems of the industrialized world as a whole. The following phenomena, some of which originated in the mid-1960s, are responsible: the U.S. balance-of-payments deficit, which has caused an enormous dollar glut on the international market; an increase in public sector expenditures, often financed by permissive monetary policy; an increase in both private and public demand that has driven prices continually upward; and the demands of labor for higher and higher wages. In Spain these problems have been compounded, ironically, by the very success of the miracle that grew on cheap fuel, easy credit, and extensive foreign

Table 12.2

Annual Growth Rate for the Gross Industrial Product, 1959-1971
(in constant pesetas)

Year	Percentage Increase
1959	0.2
1960	2.7
1961	13.6
1962	11.3
1963	12.2
1964	13.3
1965	9.4
1966	9.3
1967	4.5
1968	6.0
1969	11.4
1970	7.1
1971	3.9

Source: M. L. Ardura Calleja, "El sector industrial," in Juan Velarde
Fuertes et al., La España en los años 70 (Madrid: Editorial
Moneda y Crédito, 1973), p. 329.

Table 12.3

The Spanish Economy in 1960 and in 1970 (in millions 1970 pesetas)

	1960		1970		Average yearly growth (%)
	Value	% GNP	Value	% GNP	
GNP	1,115.3		2,252.4		8.5
Available Resources	1,193.8		2,636.0		8.2
Private Consumption	766.3	68.7	1,522.2	67.6	7.1
Public Consumption	141.8	12.7	249.5	11.1	5.8
Gross Capital Formation	177.0	15.9	521.3	23.1	11.4
Imports	78.5	7.0	383.6	17.0	17.2
Exports	108.7	9.7	343.0	15.2	12.2

Source: M.J. González, La economía política del Franquismo, 1940-1970
(Madrid: Editorial Tecnos, 1979), p. 30.

Table 12.4

Causes of the Economic Crisis: Spain and OECD Countries

Economic Indicator	Spain	OECD Countries
1. Public spending as a % of gross domestic product; variation between 1971-1973 and 1961-1963.	+42.8%	+12.0%
2. Average yearly increase of hourly wages between 1964 and 1973	14.7%	8.2%
3. Real growth rate of domestic demand in 1973	8.9%	5.4%
4. Real annual growth rate of gross industrial product for 1965-1973	6.5%	4.8%
5. Relative share of crude oil in energy consumption in 1973	66.9%	55.0%
6. Imports of petroleum products as a % of total petroleum products consumed in 1973	99.0%	70.0%

Source: La economía Española en la década de los 80 (Madrid: Alianza Editorial, 1982), p. 31.

investment. Perhaps the miracle took place too quickly and was too dependent on events that were beyond Spanish control. Table 12.4 compares the effects of these factors on Spain and on the member countries of the Organization for Economic Cooperation and Development. (OECD).

Spain is now faced with high unemployment, rampant inflation, excessive dependence on foreign energy sources, and a lack of domestic savings and investment. Spanish economists are convinced that the country cannot begin to pull out of the recession until private investment increases significantly. The percentage of gross national savings to gross national income has decreased from a high of 22.6 percent in 1973 to 19.4 percent in 1980, and the percentage of net national savings to net national income has decreased from a high of 15.8 in 1973 to 11.0 in 1980.[8] The explanation lies partly in the high cost of fuel, passed on to the consumer through higher prices that absorb more disposable income. The answer also lies partly in the continued growth of consumption irrespective of increasingly higher prices. Spain has become a consumer society, one of the consequences of the industrial revolution that began in the 1960s. It cannot be forgotten that for the first time in national history the people as a whole have money to spend and enjoy; they are now more concerned about spending today than saving for tomorrow. Their savings have dropped, and as a consequence investment has plummeted, too, from 27 percent in 1974 to 21.5 percent in 1980 (the percentage represents the ratio of gross capital formation to gross domestic product).[9] Velarde Fuertes believes that Spaniards do not appreciate just how serious the problem has become.[10] The Great Depression in the 1930s did not hit Spain as hard as it did other countries; the experience did not teach Spaniards the same sobering lessons that it taught other peoples.

In 1980, unemployment in Spain reached 12.6 percent, representing over 1.6 million unemployed out of an active work force of nearly 12.9 million. The figure in 1974 was 3.2 percent, representing 434,000 unemployed out of an active work force of almost 13.4 million. These figures compare dramatically with the years 1966 to 1969, when unemployment varied between 0.9 and 1.1 percent.[11] Most authors attribute the fall in the active work force not only to longer periods of schooling and to the lowered age of retirement but also to disillusion and disappointment among the young—many of whom have given up the search for work and have fallen back upon the family for their upkeep. In the first three months of 1981 unemployment among young people between the ages of 16 and 19 reached 40.7 percent, representing 484,000 people; between the ages of 20 and 24 the percentage was 26.9, representing 467,700 people.[12] The unemployment problem has also become more serious because more and more women are entering the work force, 29.2 percent of the population in 1980 compared to 12.1 percent in 1940 and 20.1 percent at the beginning of the economic miracle in 1959. Spanish laborers who went to work in other Western European countries and whose remunerations helped the balance of payments enormously from the mid-1960s to the mid-1970s have begun to return to Spain. Their absence helped contribute to the low figures of unemployment, but economic problems in the host countries have made life there increasingly difficult. Temporary emigration to Europe peaked in 1972 at 112,600 men and women. In 1963 the figure was 79,300; in 1979, it was 103,800. Between 1963 and 1979, close to 1.7 million people emigrated temporarily. Permanent emigration to Europe reached its highest level in 1971 at 113,700. In 1979, the figure dropped to 13,000. Between 1963 and 1979, over 1 million people emigrated permanently. Overseas emigration was at its highest in 1963 when 25,800 left Spain. In 1976, it fell to 3,200, and in 1979, to 4,200. Between 1963 and 1979 a total of 216,500 people emigrated overseas.[13]

Velarde Fuertes believes that unemployment is Spain's most serious problem not only for economic reasons but for social and political ones as well.[14] Unemployment erodes national cohesiveness. It isolates the individual and encourages the selfish pursuit of one's own well-being at whatever cost. Unemployment statistics do not always show that in some regions of the country the percentage is far higher than in others. People in depressed areas are particularly vulnerable to specious political argument, and unemployment undermines faith in the political system just when democracy is beginning to put down roots. There are those who contend that under Franco this situation would never have arisen, and that if he were alive today the situation would be corrected.

Spain had an unfavorable balance of payments in eleven of the twenty years between 1961 and 1980. Because of the OPEC price hikes that began in 1973, a favorable balance of $557 million in 1973 turned to an unfavorable balance of $3.245 billion in 1974. In 1978 and 1979 the balance was again favorable, but in 1980 the unfavorable balance was $4.989 billion, and the estimated deficit for 1981 was $5 billion.[15] Not all of the blame can be placed on the increased price of oil, but it was certainly the major factor. In 1980, 65 percent of all of the energy consumed in Spain came from petroleum, compared to 54.2 percent (1979 figure) in the nations of the European Economic Community (EEC). The percentage had declined about 7 percent from 1976 to 1980, but was still among the highest of the developed countries. Spain's domestic production of oil is almost zero; its dependence upon imported oil is almost total. The economic miracle in Spain was purchased in large part with cheap fuel, and the nation's consumption of energy is based upon petroleum products. This usage could be converted to other sources only at enormous cost and over a long period of time.

Payments to oil producers are not the sole cause of Spain's almost chronic unfavorable balance of payments. Payments for royalties and for technical assistance are inordinately high, owing to insufficient domestic scientific research and development. This situation, too, will remain relatively unchanged until the educational system and the industrial community adapt to the reality of a modern technological society. The repatriation of profits on foreign investment in Spain and interest payments on Spain's foreign debt contribute heavily to the unfavorable balance. The flow of foreign currency to counterbalance the outflow of pesetas has slackened. The tourist industry makes a formidable contribution to the national economy. In 1981 a record 40 million tourists spent approximately $7.2 billion, yet tourism is experiencing a slight decline.[16] The rate of growth has slowed, perhaps because Spain has reached a saturation point in the tourist trade. Remuneration from Spanish workers sending home paychecks in foreign currency has fallen significantly, and this situation will worsen as more and more emigrant workers return.

Inflation continues to dog the Spanish economy at a rate generally higher than in the OECD member nations. With 1960 representing the base of 100, consumer prices in 1965 were 140.6 in Spain and 112.8 in the OECD nations. In 1979 the index was 645.8 in Spain and 291.1 in the OECD nations, and the projection for 1980 was 745.7 in Spain and 326 in the OECD nations.[17]

No country will be able to solve the current worldwide economic problems in the immediate future, but care must be taken if the problem is not to worsen before it improves.

The leadership in post-Franco Spain has not paid sufficient attention to the economy, not because it lacked either interest or expertise but because politics has taken priority. Spain is only now completing the transition to democracy. The journey has been extremely difficult and oftentimes dangerous: Witness the attempted coup d'état in February 1981. Now that the Socialists have come to power and the shift from right to left has taken place peacefully, perhaps politics can for the moment be allowed to idle quietly while economics is given full throttle.

NOTES

1. Malthusian refers to the concept that the good things of life are in short supply and that one must husband the little one has out of fear that even that might be consumed too quickly. The mentality lends to a narrow, little inventive life in which risk of any sort is minimal.

2. Gabriel Jackson, *The Spanish Republic and the Civil War, 1931–1939* (Princeton, N.J.: Princeton University Press, 1965), pp. 526–540.

3. Hugh Thomas, *The Spanish Civil War* (New York: Harper & Row, 1963), pp. 631–633.

4. Ramón Tamames, *La república, la era de Franco* (Madrid: Alianza Editorial, 1973), pp. 349–358.

5. Sima Lieberman, *The Contemporary Spanish Economy: A Historical Perspective* (London: George Allen and Unwin, 1982), p. 201.

6. Since the time that the Labor Charter came into being in 1938 it had been very difficult for an employer to dismiss an employee; this protection had been guaranteed to the worker in part to compensate him for the loss of all the rights that he had possessed prior to the Charter.

7. Lieberman, *Contemporary Spanish Economy*, p. 215.

8. Servicio de Estudios, *La economía Española en la década de los 80* (Madrid: Alianza Editorial, 1982), p. 43.

9. Ibid., p. 56.

10. Juan Velarde Fuertes, "Economía," in *Cinco años después: ¿Cual es la balance?* (Barcelona: Ediciones Acervo, 1980), pp. 60–90.

11. *La economía Española*, p. 68.

12. Ibid., p. 69.

13. Ibid., p. 77.

14. Velarde Fuertes, "Economía," p. 65.

15. *La economía Española,* p. 96.

16. *The Europa Yearbook 1983: A World Survey* (London: Europa Publications, 1983), p. 1071.

17. *La economía Española,* p. 86.

13

Culture and Society

It is too early to measure precisely how deeply the Spanish people have changed with their newfound freedom. Franco has been dead for almost a decade, and the constitution that created the foundation for the new society is only six years old. But undeniably, the surface of Spanish life has changed spectacularly since the caudillo was buried in November 1975. Spaniards may now legally divorce, have abortions, smoke dope, swim naked at the beach, and openly indulge their most elaborate sexual fantasies, with pornography available at kiosks, bookshops, movie houses, and live theaters. The most prestigious newspapers—*El Pais*, for example—carry hundreds of lines of advertisements describing the charms of voluptuous boys and girls available for men and women in whatever combination tastes demand. Transvestites seem enormously popular with those who buy venereal delights, if one may judge by the number of *travestís* who advertise. Perhaps this account plays too heavily upon things sexual, but sex and politics were the two greatest taboos in Franco's Spain. Now that politics is constitutionally accessible to almost everyone, the present sensual indulgence gives evidence that there is a new Spain in the making, one that is quickly joining the mainstream of Western culture and life with all of its benefits and mischief.

SPANISH CULTURE UNDER FRANCO

The contrast to what was the officially trumpeted culture and life of the Franco regime could scarcely be more dramatic.

Spain's culture was a Catholic antique with symbols and ceremony inspired by Ferdinand and Isabella, Charles V, and Philip II. Catholic morals and ethics (and philosophy, too, to the extent that more profound elements crept into official Francoist thinking) undergirded all public life and all private life that came under the influence of the state—particularly education, whose content was almost totally shaped by the Spanish Catholic church. Foreign influences obsessed Franco, and he sought to eradicate anything that he judged had corrupted Spanish society since its heyday during the Siglo de Oro, the golden sixteenth century. Cosmopolitanism had wreaked havoc upon Spanish values. According to Franco, "the spirit of criticism and reservation is a liberal thing that has no roots in the soil of our movement, and I repeat to you once again that its tone is military and monastic and to the discipline and patriotism of the soldier must be added the faith and fervor of the man of religion."[1] Speaking of the nineteenth century—to Franco and his disciples the zenith of the "anti-Spain" that had started to take shape during the Enlightenment of the eighteenth century—Franco asked: "Doesn't a century of defeat and decadence demand a revolution? It does indeed—and a revolution in the Spanish sense that will destroy an ignominious century of foreign-inspired doctrines that have caused our death. . . . In the name of liberty, fraternity, and equality and all such liberal trivia our churches have been burned and our history destroyed."[2] In his speech announcing the creation of the FET y de las JONS, Franco recalled the Carlists in the nineteenth century as defenders of an ideal Spain against "the bastardized, Frenchified, Europeanized Spain of the liberals."[3]

These atavistic sentiments found their way into all official positions on culture and society and found expression in proregime magazines and revues like *Jerarquía, Vértice, Escorial,* and especially *Arbor,* the publication of the powerful and influential Consejo Superior de Investigaciones Científicas (CSIC, Paramount Council for Scientific Investigation), with its orthodox Catholic bias.

Franco turned his back on the mainstream of Spanish culture that had taken renewed force in the "Generation of

'98" (1898), named for the year that Spain was humbled by the United States in the Spanish-American War. The talented members of that generation sought to rediscover the indigenous roots of a once magnificent civilization, now fallen to disgrace, that might be refertilized to produce a new, authentically Spanish culture for the twentieth century. These men and women did not seek to resuscitate some epoch in Spain's past and pump it back to artificial life, as did Franco forty years later. They sought instead to rediscover in the treasure trove of Spanish history those elements that had made Spain culturally great before and that might again inspire the nation to cultural greatness.

Angel Ganivet began the national self-examination with his essay on the nature of Spanishness, *Idearium español,* published in 1896. Other notables of the Generation of '98 were Miguel de Unamuno, essayist and professor of Greek; writers Azorín (José Martínez Ruiz), Pio Baroja, Ramón del Valle Inclán; poet Antonio Machado; painter Ignacio Zuloaga; and essayist Ramiro de Maetzu, who later became a right-wing apologist. In some ways, these men followed in the spirit of their older contemporaries: Santiago Ramón y Cajal, the histologist who won the Nobel Prize for Medicine in 1906; historian Marcelino Menéndez y Pelayo; Joaquín Costa, the social and legal historian; and Pablo Iglesias, the father of Spanish socialism.

The generation that followed that of '98 took a different approach to the quest to build a Spanish culture for the twentieth century, a route that took its adventurers into Europe. The foremost name among the Europeanists, which also included Gregorio Marañon and Ramón Pérez de Ayala, was José Ortega y Gasset, whose essay, *The Revolt of the Masses,* made him internationally famous. Ortega became the lodestar for the generations of liberal intellectuals who followed him, if by liberal one means an inquisitive, restless, passionate, nondogmatic dedication to truth. Only in relatively recent years have members of the Spanish intelligentsia begun to respond to the beat of a different drum, primarily from the left. Perhaps best known of the new intellectuals is Juan Goytisolo. During the Franco years, however, Ortega the

Europeanist and Unamuno the Hispanist represented for those suffocating in the orthodox, incensed air of Francoism everything that had been and that one day might be again sublime in Spanish culture, in Ortega's words, "the iridescent gem of the Spain that could be."

It would not be fair to say that Spain under the Franco regime was a total cultural wasteland, but few of the artists, writers, and intellectuals who chose to remain in Spain achieved international recognition, whether they created within the Catholic sanctuary or outside of it. Worldwide honor went instead to those identified with the great Spanish cultural heritage who had gone abroad after the Civil War began or who were already living abroad when the war broke out and who refused to return to Spain while Franco was in power. Pablo Picasso was the most resplendent of these personalities, which also included motion picture director Luis Buñuel, cellist Pablo Casals, guitarist Andrés Segovia, and Juan Ramón Jiménez, who received the Nobel Prize for Literature in 1958 while living as an expatriate in Puerto Rico. Among those less celebrated internationally but eminent in their fields who spent many of their creative years away from Spain are historian Américo Castro, who taught at Harvard; educator Fernando de los Rios; Claudio Sánchez Albornoz; and poets Luis Cernuda and Jorge Guillén. Special mention should be made of two world-renowned artists who do not fit into the above categories. Poet and dramatist Federico García Lorca, who finally holds the place in the pantheon of Spanish greats that was denied him by Franco, was executed by the rebels early in the Civil War. For those who opposed Franco, both inside and outside of Spain, Lorca symbolized the creative Spanish spirit that had been snuffed out by the rebellion. The painter Joan Miró, after Picasso the greatest Spanish artist of the twentieth century, returned to Spain after the Civil War. He had attacked the rebels through his art early in the war and remained unrepentant. Perhaps Miró's fame protected him against reprisal, but his work was totally ignored by the regime. His country honored him, as the world had done long before, only after Franco died. At Miró's death in December 1983, he was eulogized by both king and commoner.

Freethinking intellectuals fought an uphill battle during most of the Franco years. There was some activity, however, and as the regime aged that activity became more challenging. No frontal attacks against the system were ever tolerated—the censors saw to that—and those who dared to make incursions along the flanks always ran the risk of punishment. As mentioned earlier, Antonio Tovar, the rector of the University of Salamanca, and Pedro Laín Entralgo, the rector of the University of Madrid, were both summarily removed from their posts when their voices of protest grew too bold. Had they been seen as enemies of the regime, neither would have been appointed to such exalted academic-political positions, but even these men were subject to discipline when they "forgot their place."

Some of the earliest dialogue that quietly and obliquely questioned the regime took place among progressive Catholic elite academics. In the early 1950s, Laín Entralgo and José Luis Aranguren, a distinguished professor of ethics and sociology, took part in roundtables that discussed the works of Jacques Maritain and Teilhard de Chardin, the most celebrated living exponents of liberal Catholicism. The roots of liberal Catholicism go back to the middle of the nineteenth century, and since that time its criticism of orthodox Catholicism has furnished a rich source of debate within the church and among its intellectual faithful. Joaquín Ruiz Giménez, the minister of education in Franco's fourth cabinet, also moved toward liberal Catholicism (it was he who had appointed Tóvar and Laín to their rectorships). He fell from Franco's grace in 1956 and became a part of what Juan Linz calls the alegal opposition, described in Chapter 4.

Novelists began to write critically about Spanish society, not openly against the regime as such but against the quality of life in Franco's Spain. Its ugliness and violence were described in Camilo José Cela's *La Familia de Pascual Duarte* (1943); its materialism and furtive sexuality in Cela's *La Colmena* (1951); its hypocrisy and moral putrefaction in Carmen Laforet's *Nada* (1944); its inanity and vacuity in Rafael Sánchez Ferlosio's *Jarama* (1956). In films, Luis García Berlanga and Juan Bardem tried to bring to the screen something both

Spanish and intellectually challenging, but they rowed against a powerful current of pap and fluff. The movies were (and remain) enormously popular in Spain, but during the Franco era those relatively few films that were produced domestically were either mindless musical comedies or innocuous folkloric dramas that relived in melodramatic unreality the "glorious days of Spanish history." Foreign films, particularly American films, dominated the screen, but the censors scrutinized them for a glimpse of stocking, a bit of decolletage, or an exposed thigh (a word, by the way, that was expunged by the censors from the dialogue of a stage play by José Maria Pemán). One famous incident has been told and retold. Ava Gardner in *Mogombo* was changed from Clark Gable's mistress to his sister in the dubbed dialogue of the film, in order to avoid the suggestion of adultery. The possibility of incest was obviously less shocking.

Spain has also had its share of those who created in the self-quarantined world of inner migration, what Ralf Dahrendorf calls the "romantic attitude" in describing German intellectuals.

> Here we encounter a political attitude of retreat from politics. In its hierarchy of values not only civil society but the state as well is superseded by the "true" virtues of inner perfection, of profundity, of the world of the mind. . . . Although it sentimentally deprecates reality there is no serious evaluation of the world involved in their approach; the inner emigrant is not a fighting man but likes to leave reality to its own resources in order to withdraw himself to the refuge of "truth."[4]

Those who emigrate inwardly are difficult to judge, for they obviously are able to create in any atmosphere, rendering the politics of the country in which they live unimportant to them. A person who can create while the world around him sickens is either larger or smaller than human dimension. Perhaps Miró was larger, as was Vicente Aleixandre, the poet who won the Nobel Prize for Literature in 1977. Raymond Carr and Juan Pablo Fusi believe so:

For Miró the years of Francoism were a scratch on the skin. His image of Spanish culture . . . is of a carob tree deeprooted and evergreen. The award of the Nobel Prize to Vicente Aleixandre was not merely a reward for an unsullied and outstanding talent. It was a recognition that Spanish culture had survived. Or to put it another way, it had proved impossible to cut Spain off from the modern world.[5]

POST-FRANCO CULTURE AND SOCIETY

Without doubt there is an enormous cultural output in Spain today and an enormous response to it. People are flocking to museums; the lines at the Prado sometimes seem endless. The arrival of Picasso's *Guernica,* which had hung for years in the Museum of Modern Art in New York City, was a poignant and symbolic event proudly shared by the thousands who came (and continue to come) to the building behind the Prado where the painting is housed alone in an enormous salon, protected like an icon behind bulletproof glass. The event was poignant because this masterpiece, considered to be the finest expression of the Spanish Civil War in any artistic medium, came to the land of its inspiration for the first time, and it came to stay, in accordance with Picasso's directive that it be given to Spain only after democracy had been reestablished. The event was symbolic not only because it placed the work of Picasso, considered the greatest painter of the twentieth century, in the company of Spanish immortals like Velásquez, El Greco, and Goya, but also because it marked Spain's reentry into the modern world of art.

New galleries are seemingly opening up every month in the major cities, particularly galleries that display contemporary works. It was out of the gallery of Enrique Alebo, a pioneer in exhibiting abstract art, that a painting was chosen as an official gift to the president of the United States. The choice of a work of modern art instead of something "typically Spanish" was indicative of a new artistic climate in Spain. *Ederra,* a play that treats Basque nationalism sympathetically, played to full houses at the Teatro Español in Madrid in the 1982–1983 season while Basque violence continued unabated.

The play's author, Ignacio Amestoy, won the coveted Lope de Vega prize, a striking reward for artistic freedom. The Spanish film *Volver a Empezar* (To Begin Again) won an Academy Award in the United States in 1983 and two Young Director awards at the Cannes Film Festival. Reflecting this artistic renaissance, the cultural pages of the leading newspapers in the major cities—*El Pais, Diario 16,* and others—have increased manyfold in the past few years. The Socialist government announced in November 1982 that Felipe González intended to double the budget available to the arts, and in August 1983 Minister of Culture Javier Solana stated his intention to remedy "Spain's profoundly unfair distribution of cultural goods" by introducing art and music education into Spanish schools "on the same level as mathematics." Solana also declared the Socialists' commitment to building libraries in every community with a population of 2,000 or more, in order to correct the appallingly low number of books per capita in Spain: 0.4, compared to Sweden's 4.7 books per capita, for example.[6]

All of this activity notwithstanding, it is not yet possible to say that a post-Franco culture has developed, one that will resume on a national scale the continuity of the great Spanish tradition that was almost totally interrupted during the Franco era. The great activity in contemporary Spain is oftentimes simply that: *activity.* The Spaniard is tasting, feeling, looking, reading, and hearing in an open environment after forty years of close restrictions. The men and women of post-Franco Spain are discovering themselves and shaping the kind of society out of which a new culture will emerge. In the meantime, while experimenting with everything from the most frivolous to the most serious, the Spanish people are confronting change at a speed and intensity far more accelerated than that experienced by most free societies. The issues of divorce, abortion, and the relationship between the sexes have shaken Spain to the core of its family and religious traditions, wedding for public debate Franco's two great taboos, sex and politics. The controversy surrounding educational reform has been even more traumatic, and coming to grips with the drug culture has made even those most committed to the democratic process realize just how self-destructive a free society can be.

Divorce, Abortion, Drugs

The divorce bill became law on July 20, 1981, winning against the relentless lobbying of the Catholic hierarchy and the fierce opposition of the conservative lay elite. The college of bishops issued this verdict following the bill's passage: "Rather than being a remedy for evil, divorce is converted into an open door for the generation of evil."[7] Spanish general Fernández Posse, speaking at a religious ceremony, lamented the old society that was being destroyed by new permissive legislation:

> We are at war, a special subversive dirty war. They are trying to destroy our spiritual and moral values, penetrating all our social establishments, showing the lowest tastes. . . . A stubborn enemy has infiltrated the media, the church schools and universities. . . . It seeks to propagate pernicious ideas which bring parents and children into conflict in order to destroy the family, the basic cell of all civilized society and the foundation of Christianity.[8]

Those who supported the legalization of divorce called their lay and clerical opponents hypocrites, pointing out that members of the elite had long been able to end their marriages through annulments engineered by a compliant church hierarchy. The prodivorce advocates also pointed out that the same conservative elite and the same church hierarchy had resisted earlier liberalization that struck down the jail sentence for adultery and decriminalized the sale of contraceptives. When the Socialists came to power in 1982, many articles in the civil code dealing with the relationship between the sexes remained unchanged from the Franco era. For example, under existing law, the mother of a child born out of wedlock was not allowed to establish the father's identity. A female lawyer in Madrid explained it this way: "There are many men who have illegitimate children who do not want to recognize them.

And since the Church believes in the indissolubility of marriage it would have to accept the legality of two families."[9]

It had been reckoned that between 300,000 and 500,000 couples would rush to the courts to initiate proceedings once divorce became legal. The law allows divorce by mutual consent after two years' separation. One year after the law came into effect, however, only an estimated 28,000 couples had started legal action; most couples were middle-aged, with an average of fifteen to twenty years of married life, and came primarily from the middle classes. An ironic exception to these statistics is Franco's granddaughter, Maria del Carmen, the young Duchess of Cádiz, who separated from her husband, a cousin of Juan Carlos, and started divorce proceedings.

The fact that Spaniards did not invade the courts once divorce became legal did not dissuade the opponents of abortion from asserting not only that abortion was a mortal sin but also that once abortion was allowed, demand for the operation would become epidemic. Led by the hierarchy of the Spanish church the crusaders cried out once again that the Socialists were perverting Spanish morals. The archbishop of Cuenca announced: "Assassination committed by a terrorist is less a crime than the killing of a defenseless child [fetus]."[10] In February 1983, the Spanish bishops denounced the abortion bill as "gravely unjust and totally unacceptable," and declared that abortion "could not escape the moral qualification of homicide."[11] The church put into a textbook used in parochial schools a statement that classified abortion as "a violent act comparable to terrorism and war." Another text that was not published ranked abortion with "systematic torture, concentration camps, and nuclear war."[12] The Socialist government countered that its sponsorship of permissive legislation was not changing the moral climate of Spain but was reflecting in law the changes that had already taken place. It has been estimated that before 1983 approximately 300,000 abortions a year took place in Spain and that more than 100 women died each year at the hands of bungling backstreet abortionists. According to sources in England, 75,000 Spanish women had aborted in the British Isles from 1977 to 1983.[13] The Socialists reminded their conservative opponents that upper class women historically had always had a remedy for ridding themselves of offspring produced from socially unacceptable liaisons. Article 410 of the penal code mitigated the crime of murder committed by the mother of a newly born child if the killing were perpetrated "to hide her dishonor" (*ocultar su deshonra*). Her punishment would be minimal. A lower class woman, on the other had, could not easily avail herself of this defense because by custom it was assumed that a lower class woman had no honor to protect. The Socialists removed article 410 from the code and replaced it with a new law that removes the classist insinuation but still treats infanticide committed by a distraught mother more leniently than other killings between close kin.[14]

While the debate over abortion was polarizing both the decision makers and the citizenry, the Socialist government also attempted to deal with another reality that has become part of Spanish society: drugs. In April 1983, the parliament passed legislation that made Spanish drug laws among the most lenient in Europe, altering legislation that until that time had been among the most severe. Trafficking in drugs remains a serious offense, but the possession of drugs in small quantities for personal consumption has been decriminalized. Experts predict that Spain will supplant the Netherlands as the leading drug center of Europe, and although this has not yet happened, problems related to the drug culture have multiplied. Once again, the Socialist political leaders were charged with destroying the moral fiber of the nation, an accusation countered once again by the Socialists' contention that they are attempting to handle an already existing social phenomenon and are not creating the problems through legislation. *El Pais* reported in March 1984 that until 1976, drug arrests relating to heroin distribution involved grams of the drug; since 1977 the amounts have been measured in kilograms. In 1982 the total amount of drugs confiscated weighed 109 kilos and 395 grams and the number of traffickers reached 11,000, figures similar to those for the preceding three years.[15] In 1983 there were officially 83 deaths from drug overdosage, primarily in Madrid, Bilbao, and Barcelona, and between 70 and 80 percent of armed robberies were drug related. [16] The amount of drugs consumed in Spain is not precisely known, but the amount confiscated in 1983 places Spain at the top of the list in Europe: 109 kilos of heroin and 275 kilos of cocaine.[17] In March 1984, three articles in El Pais gave some indication of the scope of drug addiction and traffic in Spain. One article concerned a twelve-year-old boy in Barcelona who was undergoing treatment; a second told of three boys—aged nine, thirteen, and sixteen—who were arrested in Granada for holding up a bookstore to get money for drugs. The third article told of a young heroin addict in San Sebastian who committed suicide after having held ten people hostage for two hours in a bank. Already there are growing demands that the government amend the recently created drug laws.

Education and the Church

If the issues of divorce, abortion, and drugs have caused a national furor, the Socialists' program for educational reform triggered an even more truculent reaction, drawing a bombardment of condemnation from the forces on the Right, captained by the Spanish Catholic hierarchy and seconded by its lay lieutenants. Bishops, priests, devout laity, and Catholic newspapers, magazines, journals, radio stations, press services, and publishing houses entered the fray. The church and its faithful were fighting a rearguard action against a secular state empowered through the ballot to bring about reforms that would change Spanish society even more profoundly than the liberalization of divorce and abortion. Responsibility for the education and socialization of the Spaniard would pass from the church and its institutions to the state and its institutions, following the pattern established in all Western democracies and breaking a tradition that had endured longer in Spain than in any other Western European nation. With only a few short-lived breaks, the education and socialization of the Spaniard had been the near exclusive preserve of the church since the days of the Catholic Kings.

The educational reform would operate at two levels: Primary and secondary education were covered by the Ley

Orgánica del Derecho a la Educación (LODE, Organic Law on the Right to an Education), and higher education was covered by the Ley de Reforma Universitaria (LRU, Law of University Reform). The level at which change would have the greatest impact, especially upon future generations, was primary and secondary education. Here the conflict swirled about the mutually contradictory guarantees in article 27 of the constitution. On the one hand, "everyone has the right to an education," and "basic education is obligatory and free." These rights would be guaranteed through a general program of instruction, and the state "inspects and sanctions the educational system in order to see that the law is fulfilled." The objective of teaching is to bring about "the full development of the human personality all the while respecting the democratic principles of social interaction and fundamental rights and liberties." On the other hand, article 27 also guarantees "freedom of instruction" to those who teach and affirms the right of parents "to have their children receive the religious and moral formation that is in keeping with the family's convictions." Moreover, "with the reservation that the principles of the constitution be respected, individuals and corporations have the right to create centers of learning," and "the public authorities are obliged to assist those centers of learning that meet all the requirements established by law."

Which of these rights take precedence? The Socialists (who had the absolute majority in the parliament) were close to unanimity in holding that the fundamental right was that of the child-student to receive the best education possible enabling him or her to meet national standards of proficiency received in an academic atmosphere committed to democratic principles. These goals would be monitored by the state and would be achieved first and foremost in the public schools. The Right was almost equally unanimous in its belief that the fundamental right belonged to the parents to have their children receive the religious and moral formation appropriate to the family's convictions. For the overwhelming majority of those on the Right, this could only occur within Catholic schools, whose right to educate as their directors and faculty saw fit and to be subventioned by the state were set forth unequivocally in the constitution. Moreover, the Right resisted even the suggestion that the state had the right to oversee the expenditures of public monies once they were granted to the private schools. During the Franco years, church schools were given carte blanche to do whatever they chose, with no requirement to give an accounting to the state. The Left did not deny that private education had a constitutional right to exist and be financially aided by the state, but the Socialists and their allies were adamant about maintaining rigorous control over all public monies that went to support private education, and about the priority given to public education. In the controversy over whose rights were paramount, the child-student's or the parents', the Socialists cited the 1982 opinion of the European Court of Human Rights, which gave precedence to the child. The Right fought fiercely to stop the passage of LODE by the Senate, introducing 4,160 amendments in an attempt to block the final vote. The filibuster action failed, and the bill became law in March 1984.

University reform was less profound in its impact on Spanish life, as relatively few Spaniards go on for higher education. Within this limited sphere, however, the changes outlined for advanced education were as radical as those for primary and secondary education. The law broke the hold of the Ministry of Education over the national university system and granted autonomy to each state university, requiring only that they follow the guidelines and meet the qualifications common to all state universities. (Private universities educate only a tiny percentage of Spaniards.) Historically, the Spanish universities had been subject to almost total control from Madrid.

Within each university, the law broke the dominance of the professoriat and within the professoriat the imperium of the *catedráticos*—the magisterial, untouchable, chaired full professors who until the reform had a stranglehold over the rest of the faculty, the curriculum, and the students. Each catedrático was a kind of feudal lord within his or her discipline, and historically, catedráticos obtained their positions through *oposiciones*, public debates among contending academics. These resembled gladitorial contests, with an official state-approved panel choosing the lone victor, whose garlands were often won more by a bravura performance than earned by quality scholarship as manifested through research, publications, and teaching.

The Law on University Reform put an end to this form of promotion and at least on paper, to the catedráticos' monopoly on decision making within the university. Their enormous prestige and resources may sustain the power of the catedráticos irrespective of the law, but in the future, all academic and administrative decisions are to be made by a *claustro constituyente* (a constituent university council) made up of catedráticos, lower-ranking faculty, administrators and staff, and for certain decisions, students. The first claustros were created on February 29, 1984, so an assessment of university reform would be premature at this point.

SPANISH CULTURE REINVENTED

For those familiar with Spain's history, particularly with the details of the country's last democratic experience during the Second Republic, the sobriety with which the Spaniards are now undergoing (enduring) change is remarkable. Even the most intense conflicts—over divorce, abortion, and educational reform—have been fought according to the rules of the democratic game. The inveterate Spanish recourse to rage has seemingly become aberrant. The attempted coup d'état in February 1981 was not successful, and the violence committed in the Basque lands or perpetrated by Basque terrorists in other parts of Spain is unacceptable even to the majority of the Basques, much less to the rest of the citizenry.

Where is the Spaniard who, according to de Madariaga, acted first and thought later?[18] What has become of the Spanish man about whom Elena de la Souchère has commented: "While he pays his respects to another through the formulas of refined courtesy custom demands of him, at that very moment the Spaniard is miles away from even conceiving of the other person's point of view."[19] Where is the Spanish stranger the trenchant hispanophile V. S. Pritchett once listened to on a train?

The whole performance illustrated the blindness of Spanish egotism. The speaker stares at you with a prolonged dramatic stare that goes through you. He stares because he is trying to get into his head the impossible proposition that you exist. He does not listen to you. He never discusses. He asserts. Only *he* exists.[20]

Where are the passionate Spaniards for whom the constraints of democracy were intolerable and where are the political doctrines into which they once poured their wrath? Where are the anarchists and the communists and the fascists? According to William Plaff, the anarchists now vote Socialist, and the Communist party has lost its appeal. What fascists still exist count for little today. The Socialists in power since 1982 are behaving more like the Social Democrats in Northern Europe than like Socialists in the other Latin nations.

Today Spain has dramatically changed. It has become a land of relentless moderation as well as capitalism, a conspiracy of modernism, enlightenment and moderation incorporating king and leaders of every party, all of them scrupulously democratic in everything they say, polite in their criticisms of others, invariably positive and constructive. It is the last thing a veteran of the Civil War might expect to find.

Possibly the Spanish have learned from history, a lucky exception among nations. Perhaps the Civil War was just too awful. Perhaps 1936 was simply another Spain, another epoch. Perhaps Franco should be credited that he put wounded Spain into a coma where everyone forgot.

Perhaps it is simply necessity. The past had to be obliterated. Spain today is a country resolutely without a memory. It has reinvented itself. For all that one might tell from the Spain of today time began on the day in 1975 when Juan Carlos became king.[21]

One is reluctant to entertain reservations about the hope for the future shared by those who know and care about Spain, but a few warnings should be offered so that too much too soon is not expected from the new democracy, either by Spaniards or non-Spaniards. Foreigners have long tended to idealize Spain and its people, beginning in the nineteenth century when "eternal" Spain was often looked at as the anodyne for the rapidly changing and in many aspects ugly new industrial world. In the present century André Malraux entitled his novel about the Spanish Civil War *Man's Hope*. Spaniards, on the other hand, often boast that their country possesses Europe's oldest democratic traditions in the ancient fueros and cortes, sources that have merely to be retapped in order for them to spring to life once again.

Spain is not a phoenix nor is it a sleeping beauty awakening unscathed by time. The country's immediate authoritarian past is far more real than its remote democratic past, and recent history augurs menacingly for the future. Spaniards lack practice in self-government and have not yet learned that democracy is not a final, reachable goal but an endless and messy process involving concessions that compromise values. Yet in the past they have swung suddenly from illusion to disillusion when they believed that their ideals had been betrayed, more often than not reacting with self-destructive political responses.

It might be unfair to dwell on the past when Spaniards are so eager to live in the present and prepare for the future, but the past must be present to caution temperance.

NOTES

1. *Palabras del Caudillo* (Madrid: Ediciones de la Vicesecretaría de Educación Popular, 1953), p. 317. The translations of Franco's words are mine.

2. Ibid., p. 54.

3. Ibid., p. 11.

4. Ralf Dahrendorf, *Society and Democracy in Germany* (New York: Doubleday, 1969) pp. 288–289.

5. Raymond Carr and Juan Pablo Fusi, *Spain: Dictatorship to Democracy* (London: George Allen and Unwin, 1979) p. 133.

6. *Los Angeles Times*, August 21, 1983.

7. *Macleans*, October 26, 1983.

8. Ibid.

9. *New York Times,* April 11, 1980.

10. *Macleans,* October 26, 1983.

11. *Diario 16,* February 5, 1983.

12. *New York Times,* October 8, 1983.

13. *Macleans,* October 26, 1983.

14. *El Pais,* October 19, 1983.

15. *El Pais,* March 22, 1984.

16. *El Pais,* March 21, 1984.

17. *El Pais,* March 27, 1984.

18. Salvador de Madariaga, *Englishmen, Frenchmen, Spaniards,* 2d ed. (New York: Hill and Wang, 1969), passim.

19. Elena de la Souchère, *An Explanation of Spain,* trans. Eleanor Ross Levieu (New York: Vintage Books, 1964), pp. 29–30.

20. V. S. Pritchett, "Spain," *Holiday* 37 (April 1965):63.

21. *Los Angeles Times,* March 20, 1983.

14

Spain in the 1980s: Things Done and to Be Done

DOMESTIC ISSUES

Felipe González has faced other problems that the UCD governments left virtually untouched. The new administration has put the approximately half a million Spanish civil servants on a continuous workday from 8 A.M. to 3 P.M., Monday through Friday, plus every third Saturday. This schedule makes it impossible for those hired by the state to hold two jobs simultaneously during the normal workday. For generations it has been an accepted way of life in Spain for workers to leave a first job early in order to arrive at a second job late (thereby often performing both jobs badly). This long overdue change, monumental in its impact on the Spanish work ethic, is only the tip of the reform that the bureaucracy must undergo. The civil service, and in particular its extraordinarily prestigious and powerful upper echelons, called *cuerpos*, which are akin to the French *grands corps*, had traditionally been almost above the control of the state. Even Franco made no fundamental changes in either the operation or the recruitment of the cuerpos, perhaps because their personnel was drawn almost exclusively from among the classic ruling elite that accepted Franco's philosophy of governing. These men and women, who often have less than a full commitment to democracy, now run the machinery of the constitutional monarchy just as they ran the machinery of the Francoist dictatorship. There are serious students of Spanish politics who contend that effective democracy will be little more than superficial until the massive power of the cuerpos has been seriously reduced.

The bill to decriminalize abortion ran into heavy fire following its introduction into the legislature, even though its provisions were moderate compared to the laws in most Western European countries. Abortion may be performed in Spain only (1) if the life or health of the mother is in grave danger; (2) if the fetus is deformed; or (3) if the pregnancy came about as a result of rape, duly reported to the authorities, or any artificial insemination not consented to by the woman. In the first two cases, the abortion may not take place later than the twenty-second week of gestation, nor may it be carried out without the approval of two doctors besides the one performing the surgery. The battle lines were drawn with the Left supporting and the Right opposing the legislation. Fraga Iribarne was totally against abortion under any conditions, arguing that abortions under certain circumstances would inevitably lead to abortion on demand. He was seconded by the Roman Catholic church and by powerful pressure groups like the National Catholic Conference of Parents of Families and Parents of Pupils. Pope John Paul II indirectly became involved in Spanish politics on behalf of the Right during his visit to Spain in November 1982, when he condemned all abortions. The Left claimed that the strategy used by the Right against the divorce bill was being retuned for use against the abortion bill. The Left declared that the Right was alleging that the law would *obligate* women to have abortions under the three classifications cited above. The Left correctly countered that the law did nothing more than decriminalize abortion for those women who choose to undergo the operation. The bill became law on October 7, 1983.

In the early fall of 1983, the Socialist government prepared to perform surgery on another sacred cow: the symbiotic relationship between church and state in education. Private schools in Spain, of which 60 percent are Catholic, educate a larger percentage of students than in any other European country except Belgium and Holland. Under the laws of the Franco regime schools that entered into contract with the state were subventioned by the state, which simply handed over the grants to the sponsoring institution, most often a church, with no restrictions. The churches usually hired teachers on a nine-month basis but received state funding on a twelve-month basis; they were free to use the remaining monies as they saw fit. The new education bill requires that all monetary aid be appropriated directly to schools that meet certain requirements and standards. In addition, the law stipulates that each recipient educational institution create a council made up of administrators, teachers, parents, and students. This council would name the director of the school, select teachers, and oversee the budget, although students would not participate in staffing decisions. For the traditionally conservative, almost authoritarian Spanish school system, and in particular the Catholic school system, the bill was nothing short of revolutionary. It was called "Eurocommunist" by its opponents, which included all political parties on the Right, the Catholic church, and pressure groups like the Association of Catholic Parents and Teachers. They declared that the bill was not only extremely leftist but anti-Catholic and unconstitutional, arguing that the law would cut funds for private education to such a degree that the schools would be unable to compete against state schools and would wither away. Supporters of the bill claimed that it was designed merely to compel all educational institutions to meet certain standards of instruction, teacher recruitment, and school management. Those schools that could or would not comply would have to manage on their own. Furthermore, private schools in areas already sufficiently covered by state schools would have their subsidies either reduced or totally taken away.

The Spanish government will have to renegotiate the Organic Law on the Harmonization of the Autonomous Regions (LOAPA), created to reconcile the differences among the autonomous regions and between them and the national government under the provisions of article 150 of the constitution. The law came into effect in June 1982, during the last weeks of the UCD government of Calvo Sotelo. It was negotiated between the UCD and the PSOE with the regionalist parties, the PCE, and some independents in bitter, often vituperative opposition. The opponents, particularly the Basques and the Catalans, maintained that the law cut deeply into the constitutionally guaranteed powers of the autonomous regions and was therefore invalid. The Constitutional Court agreed, and the González administration or its successor will have to go through the extremely controversial process all over again.

FOREIGN POLICY

Most Spaniards are eager to join the European Economic Community for both economic and political reasons. The fledgling Spanish democracy would perhaps be more secure domestically in a family of democratic nations, decreasing Spain's vulnerability to future threats against the system. Negotiations have been going on for several years, and Spain's entry seemed likely until France and, to a lesser degree, Italy had second thoughts. Agricultural products grown in Spain would compete with similar products in the other Latin nations. Portugal is also negotiating entry, and similar Portuguese products will compound the problem. Spain will increase the total farmland of the EEC by approximately 27 percent and overburden the European market with Mediterranean products. Almost three-quarters of the EEC budget already goes into the Common Agricultural Policy (CAP), a system of farm subsidies. Member nations, and especially France, believe that until the CAP has been restructured the additional surpluses from Spain could not be absorbed. During the decade that began with the oil crisis in 1973, the EEC negotiated politically sensitive trade agreements with North African and Near Eastern Mediterranean nations that also grow products similar to those grown in Spain and that have started to develop industry similar to Spanish industry. Spain's entry into the Common Market would compel a total reassessment of these agreements. Moreover, its entry is further complicated by Spain's dispute with England over Gibraltar, formerly Spanish territory. Gibraltar passed into British possession in 1713 under the terms of the Treaty of Utrecht, which ended the War of Spanish Succession, but Spain now wants it back.

Unlike other British colonies, however, where the indigenous population outnumbered the British subjects and made an unassailable argument for dispossession, the residents of Gibraltar are overwhelmingly and fiercely pro-British. In an effort to make life difficult for those who live on the Rock and demonstrate just how dependent Gibraltans are on Spain, Spain closed its border to the colony in June 1969. The people remained unmoved in their allegiance to Great Britain. In December 1982, Spain opened the frontier to allow one crossing per day, on foot. A year later, to celebrate its magnanimity, it opened the frontier to unlimited crossings for the holiday season, from December 23, 1983, to January 6, 1984. British Prime Minister Margaret Thatcher has said that Spain cannot enter the European Community until all border restrictions are lifted. Fernando Morán, the Spanish foreign minister, declared in July 1984 that the issue of Gibraltar had to be resolved since it was impossible for one Community member's territory to be the colonial possession of another. The impasse remains.

Felipe González will probably have to call a referendum regarding Spain's continued membership in NATO. In March 1982, under the premiership of Calvo Sotelo, Spain joined NATO amidst outcries (from the Left in particular) that this would jeopardize, not strengthen, Spain's security, making the nation a pawn in superpower politics. González made a campaign issue of what the PSOE considered the high-handed methods used by the UCD to push Spain into NATO while the centrists were still in power. Felipe pledged that if the Socialists won the election the Spanish people themselves would decide through referendum if they wanted their country to stay in NATO or pull out. So far, González has not called for the vote.

Most of the other problems that will confront Felipe González until his mandate expires, and that will probably vex his successors as well, should be similar to those that any European political chief faces—unemployment, recession, and inflation. The solutions for Spain can be predicted with no more surety than for any other European nation, but the discomfort suffered by Spain should not be disproportionate

crimes."[1] Perhaps the French decision came after one Socialist leader, Felipe González, asked a fellow Socialist leader, François Mitterrand, for help. Perhaps the decision came after the French saw the Spanish campaign of terror carried into France where commandos of GAL came to ferret out and kill commandos of ETA enjoying refuge on French soil. Not knowing precisely why French policy was reversed and ever mindful that the new policy could itself be reversed at any time, the Spanish government for now has an opportunity to undermine terrorist leadership and bring to Spain at least the beginnings of domestic tranquility.

NOTES

1. United Press International, September 27, 1984.

Selected Bibliography

Anderson, Charles W. *The Political Economy of Modern Spain* (Madison: University of Wisconsin Press, 1970).

Arango, E. Ramón. *The Spanish Political System: Franco's Legacy* (Boulder, Colo.: Westview Press, 1978).

Balloten, Burnett. *The Grand Camouflage* (London: Pall Mall Press, 1968).

Borkenau, Franz. *The Spanish Cockpit* (London: Faber and Faber, 1937).

Brenan, Gerald. *The Fall of Spain* (New York: Pellegrini & Cudahy, 1951).

_____. *The Spanish Labyrinth* (Cambridge, England: Cambridge University Press, 1944).

_____. *South from Granada* (New York: Farrar, Straus and Cudahy, 1957).

Carr, Raymond. *Spain, 1808–1975,* 2d ed. (London: Oxford University Press, 1966).

_____. *The Republic and the Civil War* (London: Macmillan, 1971).

_____. *Modern Spain, 1875–1980* (New York: Oxford University Press, 1980).

Carr, Raymond, and Juan Pablo Fusi. *Spain: Dictatorship to Democracy* (London: George Allen and Unwin, 1979).

Coverdale, John. *The Political Transformation of Spain After Franco* (New York: Praeger, 1979).

Crozier, Brian. *Franco* (Boston: Little, Brown, 1967).

de Esteban, Jorge, and Luis Lopéz Guerra. *La crisis del estado Franquista* (Barcelona: Editorial Labor, 1977).

_____. *El régimen constitutional Español,* 2 vols. (Barcelona: Editorial Labor, 1982).

de la Souchère, Elena. *An Explanation of Spain* (New York: Vintage Books, 1964).

de Madariaga, Salvador. *Spain: A Modern History* (New York: Praeger, 1958).

Feis, Herbert. *The Spanish Story: Franco and the Nations at War* (New York: Knopf, 1948).

Fraser, Ronald. *Tajos* (New York: Pantheon Books, 1973).

Gallo, Max. *Spain Under Franco* (New York: E. P. Dutton, 1974).

García San Miguel, Luis. *Teoría de la transición* (Madrid: Editora Nacional, 1981).

Gunther, Richard. *Public Policy in a No-Party State* (Berkeley: University of California Press, 1980).

Harrison, Joseph. *An Economic History of Spain* (New York: Holmes and Meier, 1978).

Hills, George. *Franco: The Man and His Nation* (London: Robert Hale, 1967).

Jackson, Gabriel. *The Spanish Republic and the Civil War, 1931–1939* (Princeton, N.J.: Princeton University Press, 1965).

Kenny, Michael. *A Spanish Tapestry* (Gloucester, Mass.: Peter Smith, 1969).

Lieberman, Sima. *The Contemporary Spanish Economy: A Historical Perspective* (London: George Allen and Unwin, 1982).

Malefakis, Edward E. *Agrarian Reform and Peasant Revolution in Spain: Origins of the Civil War* (New Haven, Conn.: Yale University Press, 1970).

Maravall, José. *Dictatorship and Political Dissent: Workers and Students in Franco's Spain* (New York: St. Martin's Press, 1979).

————— . *The Transition to Democracy in Spain* (New York: St. Martin's Press, 1982).

Medhurst, Kenneth. *Government in Spain: The Executive at Work* (Oxford: Pergamon Press, 1973).

Orwell, George. *Homage to Catalonia* (New York: Harcourt Brace and World, 1952).

Payne, Stanley. *Falange* (Stanford, Calif.: Stanford University Press, 1961).

————— . *Franco's Spain* (New York: Crowell, 1967).

————— . *Politics and the Military in Modern Spain* (Stanford, Calif.: Stanford University Press, 1967).

————— . *The Spanish Revolution* (New York: W. W. Norton, 1970).

————— . *A History of Spain and Portugal*, 2 vols. (Madison: University of Wisconsin Press, 1973).

Payne, Stanley, ed. *Politics and Society in Twentieth-Century Spain* (New York: New Viewpoints, 1976).

Pitt-Rivers, Julian A. *The People of the Sierra* (Chicago: University of Chicago Press, 1963).

Preston, Paul. *The Coming of the Spanish Civil War* (London: Macmillan, 1978).

Pritchett, V. S. *The Spanish Temper* (New York: Knopf, 1954).

Salisbury, William T., and James D. Theberge, eds. *Spain in the 1970s: Economics, Social Structure, Foreign Policy* (New York: Praeger, 1976).

Tamames, Ramón. *La república, la era de Franco* (Madrid: Alianza Editorial, 1973).

———. *Estructura económica de España* (Madrid: Guadiana de Publicaciones, 1976).

———. Introducción a la constitución Española (Madrid: Alianza Editorial, 1980).

Thomas, Hugh. *The Spanish Civil War* (New York: Harper & Row, 1963).

Trythall, J.W.O. *Franco* (London: Rupert Hart-Davis, 1970).

Vicens Vives, Jaime. *Approaches to the History of Spain*, trans. and ed. Joan Connelly Ullmann (Berkeley: University of California Press, 1967).

———. *An Economic History of Spain* (Princeton, N.J.: Princeton University Press, 1969).

Vilá Valentí, Juan. *La Península Ibérica* (Barcelona: Editorial Ariel, 1980).

Welles, Benjamin. *Spain, The Gentle Anarchy* (New York: Praeger, 1965).

Wright, Alison. *The Spanish Economy, 1959–1976* (London: Macmillan, 1977).

About the Book and Author

SPAIN: FROM REPRESSION TO RENEWAL
E. Ramón Arango

Set against the background of Spain's history and geography, *Spain: From Repression to Renewal* paints a detailed sociopolitical picture of Spain and Spanish culture and society from the death of Franco in November 1975 to the present. After tracing Spain's history from the earliest times to the end of the Franco regime, Dr. Arango goes on to examine Spain as it moved from dictatorship to democracy under the guidance of King Juan Carlos and his prime minister, Adolfo Suárez. He then analyzes the constitution and the centrist politics that brought it into being and describes the collapse of the center and the birth of the center/right–center/left party structure in which the political system now operates. The author looks at both the joys and difficulties of a society released from forty years of oppression and closes by outlining the problems that must still be solved before Spanish democracy and society can be secure.

E. Ramón Arango is a professor of political science at Louisiana State University, Baton Rouge. Among his publications are *The Spanish Political System: Franco's Legacy* (Westview, 1979) and *Leopold III and the Belgian Royal Question* (1964).

Index

235